Sue Breton, Dip. Clin. Psych., _____ _____ at university and was awarded her MA ____ Cardiff University for research into panic attacks. She practised as a clinical psychologist for over eight years, giving up work only to look after a large, growing family. As well as two children of her own, she has three step-children.

She returned to full-time work in 1987, and is now working freelance as a psychologist as well as pursuing several new activities, including writing fiction, sailing, bell-ringing and horse riding. Sue Breton lives in South Wales with her husband, who is a psychiatrist.

PANIC ATTACKS

A practical guide to
recognising and dealing
with feelings of panic

Sue Breton

**FOREWORD BY
ANNA RAEBURN**

VERMILION
LONDON

First published by Martin Dunitz Limited in 1986

Revised by Optima in 1995

7 9 10 8 6

This edition published in the United Kingdom in 1996 by Vermilion
an imprint of Ebury Press

Random House UK Ltd
Random House
20 Vauxhall Bridge Road
London SW1V 2SA

Random House Australia (Pty) Ltd
20 Alfred Street, Milsons Point, Sydney,
New South Wales 2061, Australia

Random House New Zealand Limited
18 Poland Road, Glenfield,
Auckland 10, New Zealand

Random House (Pty) Limited
Endulini, 5a Jubilee Road, Parktown 2193, South Africa

Random House Group Limited Reg. No. 954009

www.randomhouse.co.uk

A CIP catalogue record for this book is available from the British Library.

ISBN 0 09 181315 8

Printed and bound in Great Britain by
Mackays of Chatham PLC, Chatham, Kent

Papers used by Vermilion are natural, recyclable products made from wood
grown in sustainable forests.

CONTENTS

FOREWORD

Although there are no reliable statistics to define how many people find their anxiety disabling, we all suffer from it at one time or another, though the degree to which this affects you varies. From author Sue Breton's own experience, both as a therapist helping people to deal with panic attacks and as a sufferer herself, panic attacks are widely suffered. All too often people feel that they are freaks, that nobody else has to deal with this disorientation.

Too often people prefer to adapt their lives around their problems rather than confront what causes them. The sufferers of panic attacks are sadly even more likely to do this because they are, to use a broad generalization, often people who do not like themselves. The last thing they want to have to do is to start examining their behaviour in order to change it.

And yet those who will confront the disruption panic attacks have made upon their lives can eventually achieve control. Perhaps not complete control, but then all of us feel worried and panicky sometimes. The aim of this book is to change the role of anxiety and panic in your life from the central and most distressing feature, to the normally upsetting but bearable one it is for the rest of us. Whether you are the sufferer or witness to another's suffering, this book represents a thoughtful and concerted attack against disabling fear.

1986   ANNA RAEBURN

INTRODUCTION

This book has been written for panic attack sufferers and their families and friends. The idea of a panic attack may sound far-fetched to someone who has never experienced one, but to those who have, the fear of panicking is very real. This book sets out to bring fresh insight into the cause of panic attacks, and to give the sufferer hope and the motivation to overcome his or her fear.

Contrary to popular belief, both men and women may experience panic attacks, although more men try to escape from their symptoms by drinking excessively. Panic attack sufferers are often sensitive, intuitive, determined, self-critical people. Unfortunately, however, we also tend to be overwhelmingly negative. I say 'we' because my research into panic attacks was prompted by years of first-hand experience.

It is unusual, especially in the field of mental health, to be professionally advised by someone who has suffered the same symptoms. Yet no midwife would deny that her own experience helps her in delivering other women's babies. People who have been referred to me, sometimes after unsuccessful psychiatric treatment, often say, 'I tried to explain to the doctor exactly what it was like, but he didn't really understand. I can tell by what you say that you know exactly what a panic attack feels like.'

The advice given in this book may seem at times so basic that you wonder how it could possibly work. It may also seem very obvious, but the chances are that you have not attempted it before, or you would not be reading this now. But because the advice seems simple, don't think the course is easy – far from it. It requires determination and courage. I have often told people I've counselled that they need to work as hard at conquering their panics as they did at acquiring them in the first place. Let me give you an example.

Imagine your garden shed is in terrible disarray and you can't find anything. You dislike this state of affairs and tidy it up, but the shed will not remain tidy unless you also train yourself to put things back in their correct places each time you use them. Now, you may decide that the effort involved in making this change in behaviour is not worth it. You would rather tidy a muddled shed from time to time.

You can take a similar course of action with panic attacks. You can cope with each attack as it occurs by, for example, taking a tranquillizer. Or you can avoid the kind of situations that bring on the attack, thereby restricting your life and causing you a certain amount of inconvenience. The alternative is to work towards change. When you are motivated enough to retrain yourself – as with keeping the garden shed tidy – you'll find you are able to do it, but until you are ready to help yourself, nobody can do much for you.

If your motivation is great enough, be prepared to spend a good deal of effort in achieving your goal. You probably learned your 'skill' at panicking over a long period of time, and you can't expect to be able to change such deep-seated behaviour overnight. And it's no use trying to overcome panics because your husband, wife, mother, son or anyone else wants you to. You can only do it because *you* want to.

You might think that anyone would want to overcome panic attacks, but unfortunately this is not so. In some cases panics serve a useful purpose in the sufferer's life. They avoid even greater distress of other kinds. Sadly, some people see this as their lot. They don't think they deserve to lead a normal life.

If you want to overcome your panics, I suggest that you read this book, and give it to your family to read too, so that they know what is wrong and understand how you are trying to cope. Make notes on your progress in the charts at the end of the book, and keep the book at hand for reference until you can manage without it. *Don't Panic* is not intended as a substitute for professional help. Only you can decide whether this is necessary. If you do seek help, the advice given here should still be useful to you.

Whichever way you go about conquering your panics, remember that you are not the hapless victim of these attacks. It is in your power to overcome your fears and to stop being vulnerable – it is in your power to cure yourself.

PART I

Defining panic attacks

1

WHAT IS
A PANIC ATTACK?

Panic attacks can vary widely from person to person. The most common kind is where sufferers feel they're going to faint. The heart beats faster, palms sweat, vision blurs and there's a ringing in the ears. Some people feel as if they want to vomit, others have diarrhoea. Whatever the symptoms of an individual's attack, they're very frightening. Sufferers are afraid that people around will notice their anxiety and that they'll make fools of themselves by passing out.

Generally, subsequent panic attacks follow the pattern of the first one (see Chapter 3). Although the majority of sufferers feel they're going to faint, only a small minority actually do.

Understanding panic

Panic is a response found throughout the animal kingdom, from the smallest insect up to humans. It is best regarded as an exaggerated form of fear. Fear is an advanced state of anxiety. Panic therefore, might be regarded as very extreme anxiety. In order to understand panic better let us start by considering the role of anxiety in our everyday lives.

Much has been written and said in the media about the detrimental effects of anxiety and stress. So we tend to regard anxiety as harmful, something that we should strive to eliminate from our lives. In fact, anxiety can be put to creative use.

To most of us it is obvious that when we feel extremely anxious about doing something we are unable to do it very well. We are all too well aware, for instance, that when a word is 'on the tip of the tongue' we find it virtually impossible to recall. The harder we try the worse it becomes.

I recently had to take an employee of mine to the casualty department of our local hospital because she had been taken violently ill at work. While she was being examined, I went to give her particulars to the receptionist. I gave her Christian name, date of birth and home address, but I could not remember her surname. The harder I tried to recall it, the less likely it seemed that I would remember. I was simply too anxious. Finally, I told the receptionist I would move my car to the car park before returning to complete the form. I went outside, moved the car, and as I was walking back towards the building the name suddenly came to me.

So-called mental blocks, the plague of examination students, are an example of anxiety affecting performance. Frequently the information that has eluded the candidate returns after he or she leaves the examination room and it is all over. The apparently forgotten facts almost always spring to mind once the pressure is off, once we stop trying so hard to remember them and turn our attention to something else.

The cause of such lapses of memory is too much anxiety. An excess of anxiety can adversely affect our performance of a task. But, perhaps surprisingly, a total lack of anxiety, or too little, has a similar effect.

I know a ballet dancer who says that if she doesn't feel the right amount of anxiety before going on stage her performance is never quite as good as it might be, never quite as sharp. Similarly, a lack of pressure in ordinary life can often make doing the smallest job seem impossible. When we have plenty of time at our disposal we can't seem to get round to it. On the other hand, I have often found that the more tasks I must cram into a short space of time, the more I seem able to do – up to a point.

These last two examples demonstrate how a certain amount of anxiety is needed before we can give our best. It arouses our mental faculties, setting them at their most receptive, and centres our attention, making us concentrate on the problem in hand. Either too much or too little anxiety can impede our performance.

Flight or fight

The instinctive reaction to fear is to turn and run. Animals, and to a certain extent young children, react on this level, but as adults we have learned to defend ourselves by 'correcting' our initial responses and masking our emotions. This distortion of instinctive behaviour causes stress.

When an animal's brain registers fear, its body reacts to cope with that fear. The heart starts beating faster to circulate more oxygen to the muscles to prepare for flight. Extra adrenaline is also produced to help this surge of effort. Should flight be impossible, an animal will usually turn and fight instead. This response to fear has been termed the 'flight or fight' response.

Whenever we feel anxiety we produce more adrenaline and our minds focus on the problem in hand, cutting out whatever else is going on around us, forcing us to concentrate on coping with the anxiety. It is precisely this combination of increased adrenaline and singleness of purpose that, when experienced in fairly small doses, helps us to do our very best. The performance itself then satisfies the body's desire for a response, and calm ensues.

Any degree of anxiety requires a response of some sort from the body. Anxiety demands mental or physical action. Failure to take action in response to the bodily changes caused by anxiety – increased heart rate and adrenaline production – is stress.

Stress in a human body may be compared to the jamming of a machine. The engine continues at full throttle, but if the obstruction is not removed, the machine will quickly wear out. In the same way, stress wears out the human body before its time. When we don't act on anxiety directly, either by escaping from it or by resolving it, the necessary calm, in which the body recharges itself, never occurs. The longterm result of too much of this unresolved anxiety can be a stress-induced disease, such as a nervous breakdown or heart attack.

To sum up, it could be said that anxiety, fully expressed and satisfied, serves a desirable purpose in our lives. Exactly the right amount of anxiety is necessary to make us produce our best physical and mental performances. Too little anxiety often results in lethargy. Too much anxiety prevents us from thinking clearly. Unresolved anxiety causes stress.

Normal and abnormal panics

Excessive degrees of anxiety result in panic. Panic occurs when the usual flight response to fear is barred, or is believed to be barred. Panic might develop in a cinema that catches fire if the audience is unable to escape fast enough, or if they believe their way to escape is blocked. Panic makes people behave in ways they wouldn't in normal circumstances, or even in flight. Soldiers may disobey orders, mothers desert their children, and people trample others to death in their own fight for survival. In such instances the instinct for self-preservation overcomes all other considerations.

If the panic becomes sufficiently great and the individual is unable to take any steps to reduce the anxiety, the body eventually reaches a point at which it can take no more, and unconsciousness follows through fainting. (Of course, although anxiety can result in fainting, all fainting is not caused by anxiety.) It is commonly believed that the mind and body escape from intolerably high levels of arousal by temporarily switching off the mind – fainting.

Generally speaking, panic is regarded as normal if there is sufficient reason for it. You are trapped by a forest fire coming ever closer. The cable car hangs by a thread that threatens to break. Your car is careering out of control down a mountain road after the brakes have failed. All these situations are examples of very real threats to life and limb that the victim is unable to do anything about. Nevertheless, the desire to hold on to life prompts attempts to escape, however hopeless. Panic is non-pathological if there is a sufficiently dire situation to provoke it – usually a life-threatening one.

Panic attacks that happen, for example, in a supermarket queue, in a doctor's waiting room or sitting on a bus are not the result of normal panic. These are an extreme expression of anxiety, but what starts them off – the stimulus or trigger – is not generally regarded as life-threatening. Therefore, by definition, they are pathological. They are an over-exaggerated response to a situation.

The symptoms of a panic attack are like the body's responses to anxiety in preparation for flight or fight – increased heart rate and adrenaline production. When these are left to run uncurbed for a long time, the body becomes tired and begins to shut down in order to regenerate. The panic attack edges towards a faint. There is blurring of vision, ringing in the ears and clamminess. Few panic attack victims actually lose consciousness. Some have other symptoms, such as feelings of nausea or diarrhoea. Both of these are common responses to fear, but occur at times that would not normally be regarded as frightening enough to provoke them.

How many sufferers are there?

Because panic attacks vary in severity and frequency it isn't possible to calculate the number of sufferers with any great degree of accuracy. Those who are included in the statistics are people whose panics have become severe enough for them to seek treatment. Countless others experience the sensation of panic, after the birth of a baby, for instance, but overcome it quite naturally. Agoraphobics are one group known to have panic attacks. They form between 1 and 2 per cent of the population. Social phobics often suffer from panic attacks too. In Chapter 3 I describe how these different groups of people are affected.

A conservative estimate is that 3 per cent of the population suffers from panic attacks. So all you sufferers who were afraid to mention your problem to anyone because you thought you were odd now know you're not. There are probably other panic attack sufferers in your street, or at your place of work, who, like you, never mention their attacks because they think they're the only ones to have them.

Panic attacks are obviously caused by fear. The question that needs to be asked is, 'Fear of what?'

2
DO YOU REALLY
HAVE PANIC ATTACKS?

Is the fear you feel when a bird flies into your sitting room, or you find a spider in your bath, a panic attack? Often people who are afraid of these things have similar symptoms to the panic attacks described in the previous chapter. There are, however, very important differences. Panic attacks are the result of non-specific fears, whereas the fear of birds and the fear of spiders are obviously quite specific. Among those who suffer from non-specific fears are agoraphobics and social phobics.

Agoraphobia

An agoraphobic is someone who is afraid of some or even all of the following types of situations:

- Leaving home unaccompanied
- Going into shops, especially crowded ones such as supermarkets
- Going to public functions
- Travelling on buses
- Travelling on underground trains.

Although the word agoraphobia, literally translated from the Greek, means 'fear of the assembly or market place', the real fear of agoraphobics is not of a public place itself, but of having a panic attack in a public place, being unable to cope and making a spectacle of themselves.

Social phobia

People suffering from social phobia are afraid of meeting new people, and even sometimes of getting together with friends. They fear they will have no conversation and will appear either uninteresting or foolish. They often take refuge in heavy social drinking.

Such phobias as these are called 'non-specific phobias' because to an observer, and often even to the sufferers themselves, there doesn't appear to be any one particular thing of which they're really afraid, or, indeed, any real reason to feel fear. The circumstances that trigger fear vary widely from person to person, and the same person doesn't necessarily fear the same situations all the time. Agoraphobia and social phobia are considered more fully in the next chapter, where I describe some real cases.

Specific phobias

In contrast, a fear of a definite object is a consistent fear. Such phobias are called specific phobias because the cause of the fear is easily identifiable. Examples of the focus of fear in these specific phobias are spiders, snakes, birds, thunder, injections and dogs. Specific phobias differ from non-specific phobias in many ways.

Specific phobias are consistent. People afraid of spiders will show fear on every occasion they are confronted by one. This fear may be similar to the panic attacks already described, but with two vital differences: the fear is the direct result of the presence of the feared object, and the panic will always subside once the feared object is removed or the sufferer escapes from it. In panic attacks, however, the fear is aroused as a result of a fear of fear itself – not of some external removable object. Since the fear is internally generated, it is not as simple for the sufferer to be separated from the cause of the fear as in the case of a specific phobia.

Non-specific phobias, or rather panic attacks, are not consistent. A sufferer may or may not have an attack in a given situation on any one occasion. It depends partly on how anxious that person feels generally. Most importantly, it depends on whether the thought of panicking occurs.

This last point is central to panic attacks. A panic attack cannot happen unless the sufferer, consciously or unconsciously, plants the seed of fear in his or her own mind – the possibility that a panic attack might occur.

Therefore, if the sufferer has a low level of background anxiety, with no worries on his mind and is truly engrossed in what's going on, then the thought of panicking may not occur at all. Hence the possibility of an attack is ruled out. A specific phobic, such as a spider phobic, will not fail to be frightened on noticing a spider, no matter how engrossing surrounding events are at the time.

Treatment for specific phobias

The very easily identified source of fear, and the consistency of the fear occurring, make specific phobias easy to treat by a process known as desensitization. This involves gradually exposing the sufferers to whatever is feared, and at the same time teaching them how to relax. The rationale for this treatment is that relaxation and fear are incompatible responses. Therefore, if a person can be taught to relax in the face of fear, that fear will be overcome.

Although very successful as a treatment for specific phobias, desensitization has proved inadequate for dealing with non-specific phobias (see chapter 10). Specific phobias can be treated by the methods described for panic attacks later in this book, but these are unnecessarily complex and time-consuming for such simple disorders.

Many sufferers from specific phobias don't seek treatment. You might, for example, be afraid of spiders, but you are probably not sufficiently upset by them to feel the need to seek treatment for your phobia. It's a phobia you can live with. People usually seek treatment for a specific phobia only if that phobia threatens to disrupt their lives. For instance, a dog phobic might seek help if the new neighbours have a large dog that runs loose and makes the phobic person frightened of leaving home.

Are yours panic attacks?

If the source of your fear is something identifiable, outside of yourself, and its removal stops the symptoms of fear, then your phobia is a specific one. If, however, what you most fear is feeling faint or making a public spectacle of yourself in certain situations, then your fear is really a fear of panicking and is internally generated, caused by your own thoughts of 'What if I panic?'

Sometimes a non-specific phobia masquerades as a specific phobia. You may, for example, believe that you are afraid of buses. The very presence of a bus might make you quake. But the vast majority of people who claim to have a fear of buses are really afraid of having a panic attack while on a bus they cannot get off. This is usually the case too with those who say they're afraid of going shopping, going to the cinema, or eating out. The basic differences between specific phobias and panic attacks are shown in the table on page 18.

Because their fear is generated by the fear of panicking, panic attack sufferers sometimes panic in their own homes. Why this happens can be difficult to understand for both sufferers and outsiders. Why should people feel afraid in their own homes, where they've lived without fear for long periods? Why should they suddenly become afraid at all?

Many panic attack sufferers who feel panicky at home do so because, like Roger in Chapter 10, they feel oppressed there due to unresolved feelings towards other family members. Usually, however, panic attack sufferers tend to become panicky at home only when their background anxiety is high – when they're feeling anxious generally and when they have worries on their minds. This concept of background anxiety is explained in Chapter 5.

DIFFERENCES BETWEEN SPECIFIC PHOBIAS AND PANIC ATTACKS

Specific phobias	Panic attacks
Source of fear identifiable as external to self	Source of fear internal and self-generated, ie, a fear of fear
Always afraid each and every time phobic object appears	Inconsistent occurrence of panic depending on circumstances
Sufferers know what they're afraid of, ie, the fear is predictable	Sufferers don't know, at first, why panics happen, ie, fear is unpredictable
Can be learned as a child by modelling*	Not learned by modelling*
Easily treated by desensitization	Not effectively treated by desensitization

*see page 42 for explanation

Some panic attack sufferers begin to feel better only when a trusted companion – usually husband, wife or close friend – is with them. These companions can, without being aware of exactly what they're doing, break the panic attack spiral by taking the sufferer's mind off the symptoms, and offering comfort and reassurance. (The panic attack spiral and the way it works is described fully in Chapter 4.) For example, Suzanne, whose case is more fully detailed in Chapter 6, was afraid of having a panic attack and being unable to control it when she was alone in the house. When her fear began to get hold of her, she turned to her neighbour, a friend, whose reassurance took her mind off her fears of panicking, so that her panic subsided.

The case of Martin, described in Chapter 4, shows the remarkable insight of a sufferer into his own reasons for panicking at home, although this type of panic attack is generally more common among women sufferers.

The next question to ask is, how do people begin having panic attacks?

3
HOW DO
PANIC ATTACKS START?

The first panic attack generally forms the pattern for future attacks. To illustrate this I shall give examples of people I have treated. The three I describe in this chapter show the different forms of panic attack, although the third type is by far the most common.

> John was travelling home by bus one evening after a day out at the beach. The journey was about seventeen miles. On the way he became aware of what he termed a stomach bug, and suddenly had to go to the lavatory. He had, reluctantly, to ask the bus driver to pull in at a pub for fear of embarrassing himself on the bus.
>
> John believed this incident had occurred quite simply because of something he had eaten on the beach. It could not be helped, but the embarrassment of having to ask a busload of people to wait while he paid an emergency visit to the lavatory remained on his mind.
>
> After this he became aware of his desire to use the lavatory whenever he found himself on a bus, even on a short trip. Consequently he started to avoid bus journeys. This tended to restrict his life, since he had no car or other transport of his own.

Jill's fear of long journeys came from her worry about vomiting in a public place.

> Jill also experienced her first panic attack on a journey. She was a passenger in her husband's car as they travelled, with their two small children, to the coast for a camping holiday. On the way they got stuck in a long traffic jam. It was a very hot day and Jill began to feel nauseated.
>
> Jill had a fear of vomiting, a legacy from her first pregnancy. At that time she had suffered a great deal from morning sickness and lived in fear of suddenly vomiting in public. This fear subsided as the pregnancy

progressed and morning sickness ceased. The problem recurred more severely with her second pregnancy. This time she remained at home virtually the entire time until the birth, for fear of unexpectedly vomiting in a public place. The fear disappeared after the baby's arrival.

The first two instances of Jill's fear of vomiting were, she believed, a direct result of her pregnancy. Therefore, she thought that the symptoms would disappear once the baby was born, which they did on both occasions. Nevertheless, she retained an abnormal fear of vomiting and would fight the desire to be sick even when she was ill and when to have allowed herself to do so would have made her feel better.

In this context the fact that Jill started to feel nauseated in the traffic jam was, for her, a very frightening situation. Since they were in a traffic jam on a motorway she had no access to a bathroom. Jill felt trapped and panicked. She fought back the feelings of nausea but her heart was beating fast and her hands felt very clammy. She opened a flask and took a drink of water. The water was cool and she relaxed a little. Then she noticed that she was starting to feel better. She assumed it was a direct result of the water.

After this Jill became very reluctant to go on long car journeys. If she was absolutely unable to avoid one, she would always take water with her because she believed that a sip of it would stop the nausea. The family was accustomed to camping holidays with friends and Jill's terror of long journeys seriously disrupted their lives.

Anne was frightened of fainting in public:

One day Anne felt faint waiting at a bus stop near her home. It was a hot day and she was feeling generally unwell. Instead of getting on the bus she returned home. The following Sunday she felt faint in Mass and had to leave the church. After this she tended to feel faint not only at bus stops and in church, but also in other public places such as restaurants.

Anne led a very restricted life for about a year, then gradually started to feel better. Although the panic attacks still occurred sometimes, they did not happen every time she went out. But she only felt really safe going out in the company of another person, and hardly ever left the house alone.

The experiences of John, Jill and Anne are examples of how panic attacks can start. It is interesting to note that each of the sufferers was later afraid to return to the situation they were in when the first attack occurred – even though they were able to understand why the attack happened. John believed his diarrhoea was due to a stomach upset. Jill's fear of vomiting was a consequence of pregnancy. Anne believed she was already unwell before going to the bus stop; waiting there on a hot day had merely exaggerated her symptoms. In spite of this knowledge, all three experienced further attacks in the same situations, but could not use the physical excuses they had on the first occasion. The later attacks increased their fears because they could provide themselves with no acceptable reasons for them. Instead they became afraid of their panic attacks, which seemed to occur unpredictably and spontaneously.

In this way the sufferers came to believe that the panics could begin without warning, for no reason, and were outside their control. Since the only thing they knew for sure was that, for some reason, the attacks happened in certain situations, they came to fear those situations and avoid them as much as possible.

I have described here how John, Jill and Anne themselves believed their attacks started. The real reasons for panic attacks will be discussed later.

How is your life affected?

Because panic attack sufferers avoid situations they believe are likely to bring on an attack, some of them lead very restricted lives. Many become afraid to leave home unaccompanied, like Anne, and are labelled agoraphobic. It seems that agoraphobia and panic attacks are inextricably linked. I have never met an agoraphobic who did not experience panic attacks at the beginning. They may not actually have a panic attack for years, however, simply by avoiding situations that would provoke one.

Other sufferers from panic attacks are labelled social phobics. They are people who, for various reasons, feel inadequate in social situations, even when they are among friends. Their anxiety over how to behave and what to say makes them avoid social gatherings. Their fear of not being able to hold a conversation turns into a fear of panicking and making fools of themselves.

Children and panic attacks

Your panic attacks may not have started in adulthood. Children succumb to the same symptoms. Their panic attacks frequently occur in school, as mine did.

When I was about ten years old, one morning in school assembly I felt faint. It was a hot day. We had to stand throughout and I became nauseated when the headmistress asked us to pray for a schoolmate who was undergoing an eye operation. This first time I groped my way out of assembly with my vision blackening from the impending faint and a ringing in my ears. Once outside I was made to sit with my head between my knees and soon felt better. The teachers were very sympathetic to me.

The following day standing in assembly I began to fear the same thing would happen again. It did. I then had a few days' absence from school on the pretext of feeling unwell. In fact, I was merely too afraid to go to assembly. On my return to school the same thing happened again from time to time and my reluctance to go to school increased.

At the same time the teachers were beginning to accuse me of malingering and were becoming unsympathetic towards my panics. My concern at the reaction of the teachers to a possible panic attack only made my anxiety greater and a panic attack more likely. Eventually my parents were forced to request that I be allowed to remain alone in my classroom during assembly – a request that was somewhat grudgingly granted.

Such behaviour as I showed is frequently called school phobia. The implication of this is that the child is afraid of school. In fact, in the case of panic attack sufferers, the fear is not of school itself but of having a panic attack at school and, even more, of the attitude of the teachers to the attack.

Agoraphobia and social phobia are also often wrongly diagnosed as the cause of panic attacks. What the sufferers are really afraid of is looking ridiculous. They have become reluctant to venture into those places, or types of places, where they've had an attack before.

Many sufferers, in all probability the majority, tend to believe that their panic attacks occur spontaneously and unpredictably. They are not aware that it is they themselves who are triggering the attacks and that they have the potential to stop them. To gain control over panic attacks you have to understand fully how and why they occur where and when they do.

How panic attacks develop

The very first panic attack usually takes the form of fainting, vomiting or diarrhoea, and is often directly attributable to a physical cause. But in addition to being unpleasant in itself, the incident causes the sufferers public embarrassment and humiliation.

Following the attack, feeling embarrassed, shaken, slightly unwell, and confused, the sufferers nurture a fear that such a thing could happen again. They feel vulnerable because, not knowing exactly why it happened, they are unable to work out ways of preventing it happening again. In the meantime they convince themselves that it was some sort of freak occurrence. All is well until they find themselves in the same situation in which the attack occurred.

To clarify this I shall use Anne's experiences as an illustration of how the panic attack syndrome develops.

Anne, as described earlier, had her first panic at a bus stop. The next time she found herself at a bus stop she suddenly remembered what had happened there before and began to feel anxious. As we found out in Chapter 1, two of the initial physical responses to anxiety are increased heart rate and clamminess. These symptoms were produced and Anne started to believe that another panic attack was under way.

It is important to note that the first symptoms of a panic attack are the same as those of normal anxiety. Once Anne started believing a panic attack was in progress, on the evidence of her symptoms, she became even more afraid. This increased fear only increased the anxiety symptoms until a faint threatened. This stage was reached very quickly, and Anne immediately made for home.

Each time she set off for home she began to feel better because she had escaped from other people's gaze at the bus stop and therefore she was not so worried about making a fool of herself. Once the fear of the consequences of panicking was removed, Anne's anxiety dwindled and so did her symptoms. After such an experience, however, Anne would avoid bus stops because she believed they provoked panic attacks.

In reality this was not the case. The situations themselves were not producing the panic attacks. Anne's fear that she might panic in those situations was the real cause. Why did Anne believe she might panic? Simply because she had done so on a previous occasion.

The sequence of events goes something like this:

1. Anne would think to herself, 'I felt faint here last time. It was awful. I hope it doesn't happen again.'
2. This thought would make her anxious.
3. Her body then responded to the anxiety by increasing her heart rate.
4. Noticing these bodily reactions, Anne would think, 'Oh dear, it's starting. It's going to happen again.'
5. The belief that another fainting attack was on the way would increase her anxiety, making the symptoms even more severe.

We concluded in Chapter 1 that panic attacks are caused by fear or anxiety, and this prompted the question, 'Fear of what?' After looking at the experiences of the people discussed in the chapter, we discover that:

- John became afraid to travel on buses because there was no ready access to a lavatory. Significantly, he was not afraid to travel by train since there are lavatories on board. He was afraid of having an attack of diarrhoea in embarrassing circumstances, that is, he was afraid of his panic attacks.
- Jill was afraid of vomiting. She tended to feel sick when confined. She was afraid of panic attacks.
- Anne was afraid of passing out in public and making a spectacle of herself. Her panic attacks took the form of a feeling that she might faint. She was afraid of having a panic attack.

From these examples, we can see that panic attacks are a direct result of the sufferer's own thoughts and fears that one might occur. To take this a step further, by somehow preventing these thoughts in the first place, or by taking away the fear of panicking, the attacks can become controllable. Exactly how this may be done is fully explained in the second part of this book.

4
FROM ONE ATTACK
TO ANOTHER

Anyone who has had serious panic attacks has no doubt realized that the range of potential circumstances had gradually widened. Why should this be? Once again, let's take Anne as our example:

Anne first felt faint at the bus stop. Later, whenever she found herself at a bus stop she tended to think back to that incident and to the embarrassment it would have caused her had she actually fainted there in public. Apart from this, Anne would also recall the incident in any situation that seemed similar. For instance, it might come to mind when she was in another kind of queue, in a supermarket perhaps. If the thoughts were sufficiently anxiety-arousing to provoke a panic attack, then Anne would in future also be afraid of queuing in supermarkets.

Other associations can also trigger the memory of an attack. Anne was wearing a blue cardigan at the time of the first attack. On a later occasion, wearing the same blue cardigan, she was reminded of the original incident at the bus stop. Hence the blue cardigan had also acquired the power to produce a panic attack.

In this way, the number of places and situations in which a sufferer might experience anxiety over a panic attack widens, or becomes generalized. Those who remain indoors, the so-called agoraphobics, are often people whose panic attacks have generalized so widely that they fear almost all situations outside the home.

Ways of avoiding panics

There are often certain conditions that allow sufferers to enter a feared situation unafraid. Some can avoid panic if accompanied by a sympathetic adult, usually husband or wife, or a member of the family. The conversation and reassuring presence of the companion distracts the sufferer from the memory of the attack, and because he or she is not thinking about it, panic does not occur.

Another reason why the presence of a friend helps is that even though sufferers are aware of the likelihood of an attack, there is no fear of making an exhibition of themselves in public because there's someone with them to take care of things. Therefore the usual anxiety at the prospect of a panic attack is not aroused, and so no attack follows.

After they have successfully re-encountered a situation which they previously associated with an attack, sufferers are led to think that they'll be all right provided someone is with them. So it is very common for panic attack sufferers, and agoraphobics in particular, to be able to leave home provided someone is with them.

Other sufferers rely on different props to safeguard against attacks. Jill's case is an example. She came to believe that a sip of water would stop a panic because it had done so on the first occasion. Therefore, provided she had water with her, she believed she had the means to forestall an attack. This belief was sufficient to remove much of the anxiety involved, making an attack far less likely anyway.

Although Jill put her faith in water as a 'cure' for her panic attacks, water was, of course, not the real remedy. The effectiveness of a cure like this rests in the sufferer's belief that it will work, and in that alone. The sufferer often doesn't know why a particular cure works, merely that it does. In such circumstances it isn't surprising that one day the cure fails, leaving the sufferer more distressed than ever. One young man whom I treated provides an example of this.

Martin was a likeable twenty-year-old with a sense of humour. This was very apparent from the way he related his story. One day about four months previously he had been at the home of one of his college lecturers, along with a group of fellow students. They had been discussing their examinations. They were all drinking coffee when, Martin told me, his hands began to shake slightly for no reason whatsoever. The cup and saucer he was holding rattled and he was forced to put them down. He was very embarrassed. Following this, Martin had a similar problem in the bar. Suddenly, for no apparent reason, his hand trembled when he picked up his glass. Thinking this might be due to nerves, Martin bought himself a brandy. He sipped the brandy and the shaking eased. Martin then adopted the belief that a sip of brandy was the antidote to the shaking hand. He started carrying a small hip flask of brandy with him whenever he went out.

All was well for several weeks. Unfortunately, one day his antidote failed him. The shaking didn't stop. Martin became despondent and remained at home for some days pondering his plight. He was considering seeking medical advice for what appeared to him a ridiculous problem when the thought crossed his mind that he might even be vulnerable to these attacks at home, where he felt most secure. No sooner had this occurred to him than his hand began to shake and he decided that the problem had gone far enough. 'I knew then that I had to get outside help no matter how ridiculous it seemed.'

Martin's case illustrates admirably that these cures by association are very precarious. It requires only a slight doubt as to their effectiveness in the mind of the sufferer for their power to prevent or forestall an attack to be lost.

The panic attack spiral

As has been mentioned previously, panic attacks are the result of anxiety or fear. The fear that arouses them is the very possibility of having an attack in a confining or public place. It becomes clear that the fear of panicking itself brings on the symptoms of the panic attack. These early symptoms then increase the sufferer's fears and the attack progresses. This pattern continues until the sufferer manages to escape from the situation, reducing his anxiety about making a public spectacle of himself. This pattern of increasing fears and attacks is called the panic attack spiral.

Sufferers break the panic attack spiral when they start thinking that their panic is under control. Those who use antidotes such as Jill's sip of water or Martin's sip of brandy firmly believe that these remedies will cause their panics to subside. Believing this, they feel less afraid and so the symptoms produced by the panic attack die away.

The same happens once sufferers know they're safe from public scrutiny, for example if they leave the supermarket or a room full of people to sit in the car or return home. Once they no longer feel trapped or confined they stop being afraid of losing control. If they are unobserved, it often does not matter if a panic attack happens.

There are, however, certain circumstances in which sufferers can panic alone in their own homes, and these I will describe in Chapters 7 and 15.

The thought sparks the attack

It's that fleeting thought 'What if I panic now?' that sets the whole panic attack spiral in motion. Without this thought – and it can be so brief that the sufferer is unaware of it until taught to watch out for it – the panic won't start. Panic attack sufferers bring on their own panics by their own thoughts. Therefore the control lies entirely with them. If they don't have the thoughts, they won't panic.

This is all very well in theory. In practice, the thought that triggers a panic attack is very hard to bring under control, as the vast number of sufferers

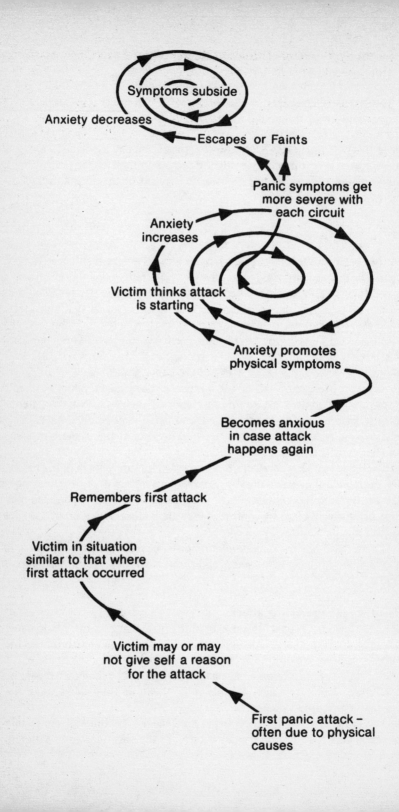

can testify. If control of panic attacks were easy, then nobody, or very few people, would be suffering from them.

The sequence of events in a panic attack, as I have explained it so far, is shown opposite. You need to understand this sequence fully before proceeding to deal with your attacks. Re-read this chapter carefully if you are not sure you understand the sequence.

5

ANXIETY: ITS PART IN PANIC ATTACKS

Although we all experience anxiety at different times in varying degrees, we don't all have panic attacks. Most sufferers would like an answer to the question, 'Why me?'

The part played by anxiety in the build-up to a panic attack has already been described. There are, however, different types of anxiety and it is important to distinguish between them when trying to understand panic attacks.

Trait anxiety

Our traits of character are relatively permanent attributes that distinguish us from other people. They may be inherited or developed during early life, and they become an integral part of our personalities.

If you describe a person as patient, you mean that person is remarkably more patient than the next. Generally we describe someone's personality by those traits that mark them out. For example, we all do both good and bad things at various times. We would describe people as being predominantly good or bad only if they are more noticeably that way than the majority of us.

A trait is a relatively enduring feature of an individual's personality. Though we are all different, we tend to behave consistently and it is our personality traits that make for this consistency. When we hear of someone acting 'out of character', it usually indicates that they haven't behaved in the way we've come to expect of them according to their traits.

A tendency to become anxious easily is as much a personality trait as patience or impatience. People with this trait are probably more likely to succumb to panic attacks, although there is, as yet, no firm evidence of this. Panic attack sufferers seem to have certain personality traits and tendencies in common. I shall return to these in Chapter 8. For now let us content ourselves with the fact that panic attack sufferers are probably more liable to become anxious than the mythical average person. Happy-go-lucky, easy going people don't get panic attacks.

Trait anxiety
A personality trait of someone who becomes anxious much more often and much more readily than the average person.

State anxiety
The feeling of anxiety that any one of us may experience in certain situations, and which goes away once the situation has passed. For example, you feel anxious sitting in the dentist's waiting room, but your anxiety has gone by the time you leave the surgery.

Background anxiety
This is a constant nagging feeling of uneasiness or anxiety, usually relating to an unsatisfactory aspect of the sufferer's life. Typical causes of background anxiety are the threat of losing one's job, an ailing marriage, the recent death of a loved one, or a sick child. Background anxiety is usually caused by something that the people experiencing it can do little to change. They have to sit it out and wait for things to resolve themselves in the course of time. Background anxiety alone doesn't provoke panic attacks but when added to state anxiety in a particular situation, it can increase the anxiety sufficiently to provoke panic.

Acute anxiety state
This is a psychiatric condition in which people suffer from such severe anxiety that they feel continually agitated and tense, depressed and unable to sleep, and unable to cope with everyday life. It is not, however, a permanent state. Panic attacks may be a feature of this condition but instances of panic attacks alone don't constitute an acute anxiety state.

State anxiety
A person doesn't have to be anxious by nature in order to experience state anxiety, although the two are often closely related. State anxiety, as the name implies, is an occasional anxiety felt, for example, just before a driving test or an interview. To clarify this difference let's take an example.

Imagine a person you would describe as a 'miserable old so-and-so'. Picture this same person receiving the news that he has won a lottery. He feels happy. This is the state of happiness, the mood of the moment – and it will pass. So too with state anxiety. It's a relatively brief feeling in response to a certain situation. It will go away when the problem causing it is resolved.

The anxiety that causes panic attacks is state anxiety – it is brought on by a certain combination of circumstances that can be resolved, and once it is resolved, the anxiety will go away.

Background anxiety and acute anxiety state

Although the panic attack is triggered by state anxiety, the sufferer may also be a victim of background anxiety. If someone has a nagging worry at the back of his mind – for example, that he might lose his job – this is background anxiety. It heightens state anxiety and contributes to panic attacks.

Acute anxiety state is a continuous high level of state anxiety, and differs from it in that it is constant, though not permanent, whereas plain state anxiety soon passes.

6
PATTERNS
OF PANIC ATTACKS

Panic attacks can take one of four forms. If you are, or have been, a panic attack sufferer, you will undoubtedly fall into one of the following categories; try to decide which one as you read the descriptions. Should you still be uncertain after that, there is a questionnaire at the end of this chapter to help you.

Acute-only attacks

Walter was forty-five years old, married with two adolescent children. He had been working as a sales representative for seventeen years, until he lost his job as a direct result of his panic attacks.

He said that for some eighteen months before losing his job he had been feeling anxious all the time about nothing in particular. He had gone to see his family doctor, who prescribed tranquillizers. These didn't help. Instead Walter started drinking more, as he found relief this way. He was drinking eight or nine pints of beer a day.

Walter's first panic attack occurred about seven months after he had complained to his doctor about his general anxiety. Every Sunday he had to take his wife to visit some relatives. He didn't look forward to these outings. In addition to his background anxiety, these visits provided specific anxiety. One Sunday evening at his sister-in-law's home Walter suddenly felt what he described as vibrations through his head and body. He felt dizzy. A doctor was called and diagnosed severe tension. He prescribed further tranquillizers.

After this, Walter began to experience panic attacks at work. His job required him to visit various small shops to sell his firm's products. While negotiating a sale he would feel a panic attack starting and would have to leave the shop and escape to his car. Naturally, such behaviour soon resulted in a marked drop in sales, and eventually he was dismissed.

Once he had lost his job, Walter became afraid to go anywhere in case he had a panic attack – with one exception. He found a public bar eight miles from his home where he felt safe. He described it as his 'escape from reality'. He had never before visited this bar so it held no association with his everyday anxieties. He was able to relax there and leave his worries behind him.

Walter's acute-only type of panic attacks are associated with a high level of non-specific background anxiety that the sufferer might not always be aware of. The anxiety is apparent as a vague but constant feeling of unease, and often has its roots in a minor worry that has been suppressed and has grown out of all proportion.

Acute phases of panic attacks build up gradually from the first one to a point where the sufferer's normal daily life is severely restricted.

Jane's acute panic attacks developed as a result of suppressed anxiety following the death of a very close friend in a car accident. Jane had always had a secret fear of being involved in such an accident herself. When it happened to her friend, it made her fears more real, but she pushed them to the back of her mind and tried to ignore them.

One night she was in a car on a motorway when she suddenly broke down, overcome by her fear of accidents and the memory of her friend's death.

Of course not everyone suffering from suppressed anxiety will end up with an acute phase of panic attacks. Many other factors are involved. Even so, anyone with constant unresolved anxiety should consider seeking professional help. To be incessantly anxious about a situation that shows no signs of improvement is not healthy in the long term. The very acute phase of panic attacks generally requires professional treatment, at least from your family doctor. Suzanne's case is an example of chronic anxiety leading to very acute panic attacks.

Suzanne and her husband moved over two hundred miles away from her home on account of his job, to a very depressed and unstimulating part of the country, where Suzanne felt an outsider and, moreover, bored. She had a panic attack one day at a bus stop. The attacks began to happen in more and more places. She became afraid to go out. Finally she started having attacks at home.

Suzanne was extremely depressed as well as being in a state of almost constant agitated anxiety. In this condition she was unable to think things out clearly and a course of tranquillizers was prescribed to alleviate her distress initially. Then she might take an active part in her recovery.

Suzanne did overcome her panics, as did Walter and Jane, by following the treatment outlined in this book.

As I noted earlier, there are four forms of panic attacks. The acute phase is by far the most serious and most distressing. At the other end of the spectrum is the spasmodic attack. The table below explains their relationships.

RELATIONSHIP BETWEEN SPASMODIC AND ACUTE PHASES OF PANIC ATTACKS

Acute phase .... Spasmodic phase

Background anxiety becomes less as you move along this continuum from left to right. Panic attacks become less generalized and less frequent.

Acute phase	Spasmodic phase
• This is the most disabling and severe form of panic attacks	• Least disabling phase of panic attacks
• Anxiety is almost constantly high	• Sufferer may have experienced acute phase in the past. Now tends to get panicky only in a few unusual situations, or if feeling particularly anxious from time to time
• Panics occur in so many different places that the sufferer is virtually restricted to staying at home	
• May even have panic attacks in the home	
May need professional help initially	*Can be self-treated with sufficient motivation*

Between these two extremes are other stages with varying mixtures of acute and spasmodic severity. Sufferers may progress from the acute to the spasmodic phase if they experience a reduction in background anxiety. They may progress from the spasmodic to the acute phase if they find themselves confronted with intolerable degrees of unavoidable anxiety.

Spasmodic-only attacks

People who have spasmodic-only attacks are rarely seen by doctors. This is probably because those who have them never feel that their attacks are enough of a problem to need medical attention. Judging by the number of people who have told me in the course of my research that they have had an occasional panic attack, a sizable percentage of the general population falls into this category.

People who experience spasmodic attacks do not generally suffer from high background anxiety. Their attacks are usually the result of excessive anxiety associated with a specific occasion. Sufferers enter similar situations reluctantly, but find they can cope with their fears.

People who experience a series of spasmodic attacks, like Marian in my next case story, have a recurring tendency to panic. Unfortunately, like Marian, they are not always motivated enough to seek out the true cause.

Marian's attacks occurred at several points in her life. On the last occasion she attributed them to her husband's redundancy. Once her husband found a job, Marian believed that her attacks would disappear – which they did.

Marian was thirty-five years old and lived with her husband and four children aged between twelve and fifteen. She worked part-time as a domestic. Her first panic attack occurred when a dog jumped on her as a child. She said she remembered becoming hot and sweaty with a floaty feeling. Although she didn't develop a fear of dogs, the memory of the panic stayed with her.

After her youngest child was born, Marian started to experience bouts of these same feelings of panic – but now there was no recognizable cause. She became reluctant to go out alone. There was, however, a friend who was prepared to accompany her wherever she went and this, along with tranquillizers prescribed by her family doctor, brought a temporary end to the disorder.

The attacks started again when her husband lost his job. Again Marian became afraid to leave the house unaccompanied, but by the time she came to see me, her husband had got a new job and she was feeling better. She failed to keep further appointments for treatment. As far as she was concerned her panics ceased to be a problem.

Marian's case is typical of people who tend to experience panic attacks when they become worried over something. She didn't seem to be unduly upset that these attacks kept returning, as long as they disappeared again once her anxiety had been resolved.

Many sufferers like Marian are content to rely on tranquillizers to help them over their attacks. But these, as we have seen, are only a temporary measure, and not a real cure.

Another case of spasmodic panic attacks involves a friend of mine.

When Gaynor was nine, she was at a children's service in church with her sister. She suddenly felt she needed to go to the lavatory but was afraid to ask to leave the church. She wet her knickers and still remembers the extreme embarrassment at getting up from the pew and leaving a puddle behind.

Many years later when she was training as a policewoman, she began to notice a desire to go to the lavatory during lectures, but only at times when she felt unable to get up and go. If she was free to leave without causing a stir, the feelings didn't arise.

She managed to control the urge by drinking little and going to the lavatory between lectures. The problem disappeared until she had to go to court to give evidence. She began to be afraid she would want to go to the lavatory when she was in the witness box.

This worried her and she discussed it with me. I was able to show her that the cause of her problem was her fear of embarrassment. I pointed out that she became afraid only when she realized it wasn't convenient for her to go to the lavatory. She should be firm with herself and stop thinking about it. She should try to keep her mind on other things and to ignore the feelings. Fortunately she had the courage to follow my advice and found that it worked.

Between acute-only and spadmodic-only cases lie the remaining two types of attack. The first of these is acute-spasmodic.

Acute-spasmodic attacks

As the name implies, these attacks begin with a typical acute phase as described above. The acute phase gradually disappears over a period of weeks or months, due to the removal of the high level of background anxiety. Sometimes this is achieved because the sufferer is successful in avoiding all those situations that tend to bring on an attack.

Many housewives who are labelled agoraphobics have confined themselves to home after a series of acute panic attacks. As time goes by and their fears lessen, they are able to go out accompanied by a close friend or relative. The high background anxiety that was responsible for the initial acute phase of attacks has subsided. At this stage sufferers experience a panic attack only if, for some reason, they are feeling particularly anxious, or if they have to go out in circumstances that cause them to fear a panic

```
                  ┌─────────────────────┐
                  │   Do you have panic │
                  │       attacks?      │
                  └─────────────────────┘
                            │ Yes
  ┌──────────────────────────────────────────────────┐
  │  Are you severely restricted                      │
  │  by your panics so you're                         │  Yes
  │  very afraid to do normal                         ├──►
  │  things, eg, stay home alone,                     │
  │  go to work?                                      │
  └──────────────────────────────────────────────────┘
                            │ No
  ┌──────────────────────────────────────────────────┐
  │  Have you ever been                               │
  │  restricted like this at any                      │
  │  stage in the past?                               │
  └──────────────────────────────────────────────────┘
                            │ No
  ┌──────────────────────────────────────────────────┐
  │  Do you have panics from                          │
  │  time to time?                                    │
  └──────────────────────────────────────────────────┘
           │ Yes                │ No
  ┌──────────────────┐
  │   Spasmodic      │
  └──────────────────┘
  ┌──────────────────────────────────────────────────┐
  │  Because you have answered                        │
  │  the last three questions in                      │
  │  the negative it is unlikely                      │
  │  that you suffer from panic                       │
  │  attacks                                          │
  └──────────────────────────────────────────────────┘
```

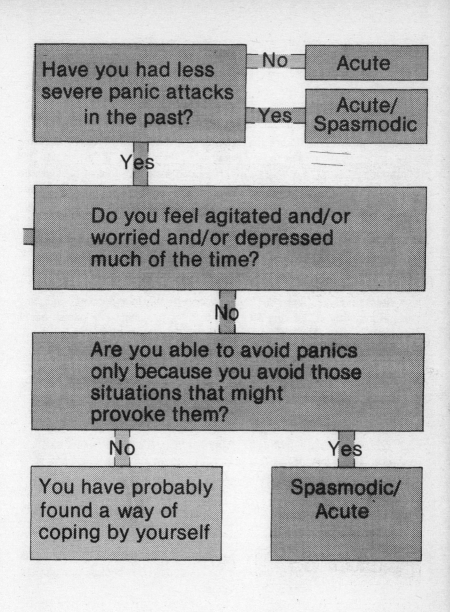

Have you had less severe panic attacks in the past?

No → Acute

Yes → Acute/Spasmodic

Yes ↓

Do you feel agitated and/or worried and/or depressed much of the time?

No ↓

Are you able to avoid panics only because you avoid those situations that might provoke them?

No → You have probably found a way of coping by yourself

Yes → Spasmodic/Acute

What type of sufferer are you?
Find your way along the chart according to whether you answer 'yes' or 'no' to each question.

attack. Believing that the worst has passed, acute-spasmodics do not always bother to seek treatment unless they find themselves once again in an acute phase.

Spasmodic-acute attacks

Spasmodic attack sufferers can do a lot to prevent acute attacks by avoiding the situations they know to be dangerous to themselves. If they can do this without restricting day-to-day life, they can also stay free of background anxiety. If they change their lifestyle because they live in fear of panic attacks, background anxiety will build up and make the attacks more likely.

People suffering spasmodic-acute attacks are those who have experienced spasmodic attacks over a fairly long period, sometimes several years. Suddenly their level of background anxiety is raised, perhaps by a deeply disturbing event such as the death of a close relative, or redundancy.

Alternatively, sufferers suddenly become unable to avoid panic-inducing situations without drawing attention to their problem. The panics occur more frequently. The sufferers then become even more anxious as a result and lapse into the acute state. The case of Alan demonstrates this.

Alan was twenty-eight years old. He was married, with two young children, and had a job as a teleprinter tester. For three years he had noticed that he became very tense when he took the family on holiday, and could relax only on their return home.

Six weeks before coming to see me for help, Alan had a panic attack at work. There had been a big argument between management and shop floor, and angry words were exchanged. Alan had become anxious and panicky during the confrontation. After this he was subject to panic attacks whenever he went out, especially in company. Attacks also threatened at work, particularly, Alan noticed, when he was not very busy.

Alan's panics rapidly developed into an acute phase because he was unable to avoid going to work, which created greater background anxiety and raised his susceptibility to panic.

Although a tendency to become anxious easily obviously makes a person more vulnerable to developing panic attacks, it is only with true state anxiety (see Chapter 5) that they occur. State anxiety may be very brief, in which case spasmodic panic attacks result.

If this anxiety grows and becomes more pervasive, the sufferer feels at best generally uneasy, at worst downright afraid. Beset by fear, he or she is prone to an acute phase of panic attacks. The course of attacks may change along with the state anxiety. A sufferer may experience any combination from the easily forgettable spasmodic-only attacks to the almost intolerable acute phase.

Panic attacks often seem to disappear without treatment, as we shall see in Chapter 8, but they only *seem* to disappear. If deep-seated anxiety is ignored, it won't go away. It is necessary for the sufferer to confront anxiety in order to conquer it. And though panic attacks are not possible without anxiety, it is possible to get to grips with anxiety without inducing a panic attack. That is the aim of the treatment for panic attacks.

7
HOW YOU RELATE TO OTHER PEOPLE

It was suggested in Chapter 5 that a tendency to anxiety may be hereditary, but there is no evidence to suggest that agoraphobia and social phobia have any directly inherited cause. Panic attacks are not passed down from one generation to the next, and if you suffer from panic, there is no need to suppose that your children will suffer too.

Two major influences shape our lives, our heredity and our environment. Although heredity does not seem to play a part in a person's susceptibility to panic attacks, the same cannot be said of environment.

The modelling process

It has been found that people who suffer from the more common specific fears of spiders, snakes and thunder, for example, have a close relative, usually a parent, who also shares that fear. There is a natural instinct in young mammals to copy the behaviour of their parents. By this process they learn to survive. This copying is called modelling. It isn't surprising then that a child, seeing its parent display fear of certain things, may well learn to fear those things too. In this way the phobia passes from parent to child.

A child may also model itself on a non-phobic parent. A phobic parent may also take great pains to ensure that a child is unaware of the phobia by trying to hide the symptoms, and so avoid the chance for modelling to occur.

Specific phobias are not acquired only by modelling. It is quite common for a child to develop a phobia of something due to other circumstances. Fear of dogs is a good example. Often a child may develop such a fear after having been bitten or frightened by a dog. Modelling in such circumstances may reverse the phobia if the parents deliberately display their love of dogs and absence of fear of them to the child. Similar tactics can be applied to other specific phobias.

If a phobia is to be developed by modelling, the child has to be aware of what the parent is afraid of. In the case of thunder, spiders and the other specific phobias, this is usually obvious. The connection is far more obscure in the case of panic attacks.

As was shown in Chapter 4, panic attacks are perpetuated by fear of a repeat attack. This is a fear that grows in the mind of the sufferer, and isn't easily observed or understood by an onlooker. Therefore a child is unlikely to copy panic behaviour, and in fact there is little evidence of panic attacks among children of sufferers. Even so, in Chapter 16 I shall suggest ways in which sufferers can take precautions against teaching the disorder to their children.

Children do, of course, have panic attacks. These develop for much the same reasons, and in the same way, as they do in adults, rather than as the result of the children having modelled themselves on the behaviour of someone else (see also Chapter 16).

Direct influence of significant others

Leaving aside the question of heredity and modelling, significant people in our lives – including parents and children, as well as other people we care about at home and at work – can have a direct influence upon the development of panic attacks. These influences are generally unpremeditated. I have never come across a case where a close relative or friend deliberately exacerbated a sufferer's panic attacks, but a crisis can be brought about by friction between two people, or when one person is over-anxious about another.

Sufferers in the acute phase are most susceptible to the behaviour of people who matter in their lives – 'significant others'. This susceptibility contributes to the sufferer's raised background anxiety level, making panic attacks more likely. The case of Betty, whose husband not only failed to sympathize with her panic attacks, but was openly hostile towards her because of them, is a fine example of this type of vicious circle.

Betty was forty-two years old and lived with her husband and four children aged between two and eleven. She worked part-time as a cleaner. Her first real panic had occurred only six weeks before I saw her, but she said she had been having problems since the birth of her youngest child. She had started wanting to avoid people, although she had continued with her cleaning job. Her first panic came over her suddenly while she was standing in her kitchen. She said she'd suddenly become confused. After this, her fear of meeting people in the street increased. She even panicked on meeting her sister. She became afraid to go out, stopped doing the housework, and lay on the couch all day. Finally she was admitted to hospital, where she said she felt better able to relax.

Although it was obvious that Betty was in an acute phase of panic attacks, it wasn't immediately obvious what was causing her high level of anxiety. This anxiety had presumably increased since the birth of her fourth child. It is not uncommon for women to report the onset of panic attacks following the birth of a baby. The great responsibility and being in constant demand can make an overworked, ever-weary new mother very vulnerable. Once a panic occurs, the anxiety increases even more.

In Betty's case the additional responsibility of looking after the fourth child had become unbearable because of the lack of support from her husband. He had become openly hostile towards her, and the more incapacitated she became, the more hostile he was. This hostility and lack of emotional support only accentuated Betty's anxiety, making matters worse. Once in hospital and out of the hostility-anxiety cycle she began to relax and feel better.

The problems returned as soon as Betty went home for the weekend. Her husband left her alone with the children and went out almost the entire time she was there. On her return to hospital Betty announced that she was contemplating divorce.

Having made that decision, it was almost as if Betty were able to stop worrying about her husband's behaviour towards her. She managed to break the vicious circle whereby her husband's hostility had increased her anxiety, making her panicky and increasing his hostility.

After her discharge from hospital Betty announced that, no longer afraid of his reactions, she had discussed her feelings with her husband. It appeared that he had not taken her illness seriously, believing she could 'pull herself together'. His leaving her alone had been a clumsy attempt on his part to make her cope – but it had in fact had the opposite effect. Having now discussed their feelings and the situation, Betty and her husband reached a new understanding and were reconciled.

Betty's case serves to illustrate the point that well-intentioned actions by interested parties can often misfire very badly. The best policy to adopt is to ask what the other person intends by his behaviour and to explain one's own.

It isn't unusual to find close relatives of panic attack sufferers becoming hostile. This is usually because they're confused. They see someone they care about suffering and are unable either to understand the cause or to do anything to help. In such a situation their frustration may unwittingly turn to hostility and anger. Unfortunately this often has the worst possible effect, increasing the anxiety of the sufferer. This difficulty is more fully discussed in Chapter 17, where ways of dealing with it are suggested.

We have looked here at the part that may be played by friends and relations in the development of panic attacks. Their influence alone isn't usually sufficient to provoke an attack. It is not the fault of others that a person has panic attacks. The fault, if indeed there is one, must lie with the sufferer. The actions of others can only exacerbate a situation that already exists, not cause it.

Indirect influence of significant others

Significant others can indirectly influence the sufferer of panic attacks if he or she feels guilty that the attacks are causing others distress. The significant others become, through no fault of their own, a source of anxiety to the sufferer, whose suffering therefore increases.

The anxiety Jill felt about becoming panicky in the car (Chapter 3) was increased because she feared her sons would become agitated by her behaviour and might even start having panic attacks too. Alan, who was mentioned in Chapter 6, increased his chances of becoming panicky on holiday because he was concerned lest his panics should prevent his wife and children from enjoying themselves.

There is nothing to be gained by a panic attack sufferer worrying about the consequences of the panic attacks for others, since, in the end, this will make coping more difficult. Concern for others will be beneficial only if it is sufficiently powerful to provide the total motivation for overcoming the panic. Such motivation is extremely rare on a day-to-day basis. It may occur if the sufferer perceives a loved one's life to be in danger. For instance, a mother who is afraid of leaving home might do so on the spur of the moment to prevent her child running into the path of a car. But this would not constitute overcoming a panic attack. For a panic attack to occur, there has to be a fear of panicking. In the situation just described the fear would not have the opportunity to surface, since the mother's only concern at that moment would be for the safety of her child.

Excessive worry over the plight of a member of the family can raise the background anxiety of someone inclined to panic attacks sufficiently to provoke an acute phase. Mothers may tend to feel uneasy over sick children, husbands may worry about how to cope if wives are ill, parents may worry over a child's future. Worries of this sort create anxiety in most people. To those liable to panic attacks they present a far greater threat until the sufferer learns how to cope with that anxiety and defuse it. Ways of doing this are described in Chapter 14.

It is very important that both panic attack sufferers and their relatives and friends should discuss exactly how they feel about their respective roles in a positive way and with a view to helping one another, rather than shouting complaints and accusations. If both parties are honest, the sufferer will often find that beneath the hostility there is a genuine concern and desire to help. And the person who is hostile, through fear and misunderstanding of the sufferer's complaint, will come to realize what is wrong and offer positive support.

8
FACING UP TO YOURSELF

It should by now be obvious that if you have panic attacks they occur as a direct result of your thoughts and feelings. Therefore, by definition, they must be regarded as self-inflicted. 'Well,' you might say, 'I couldn't help it that my mother died and I was worried about going into hospital.' Maybe not. But others have faced the same problems, probably worse ones, and survived without panic attacks.

Although we panic sufferers may have numerous sterling qualities, we also have negative ones, and it is these that lead us towards panic attacks. To ignore this would be to bury our heads in the sand. The time has come to confront our defects in order to take steps to remedy them. There's no lasting cure for panic attacks save the honest resolve of the sufferer. That resolve may falter from time to time, but if it keeps returning it will eventually be rewarded.

Punishment or reward?

Most people believe that it's better to mould the behaviour of a child by rewarding it when it does well, rather than by punishing it for doing wrong. Unfortunately, children do not always respond to this treatment. Although some children learn by being rewarded and encouraged – positive reinforcement, as it's called – others learn best from their mistakes – negative reinforcement. They will make a greater effort to avoid repetition of an unpleasant experience than they will to repeat a very pleasant one.

Panic attack sufferers appear, generally speaking, to respond better to negative reinforcement. They will do almost anything to avoid the possibility of further very unpleasant panic attacks, even if it means that by doing so they miss out on some potentially enjoyable experiences. Panic attack sufferers appear to thwart their own enjoyment of life.

It has also been found that panic attack sufferers show abnormally high feelings of general hostility, which they direct mainly at themselves rather than at other people. They tend to be very angry with themselves, blame themselves, believe themselves to be unworthy and undeserving of good things in life. This attitude is often a problem in encouraging them to overcome their panics.

Panic attack sufferers find they are torn in two by their dilemma – although part of them wants to enjoy life again, another part tells them that they don't deserve to. As a result, they get into the habit of putting off the effort required to get back into the swing of normal life. Even when they have the power to overcome their panics, they hold back for no better reason than the thought that tomorrow will do just as well. They are afraid to be happy. A similar dilemma is experienced by eternal dieters. They dislike being overweight, are disgusted with themselves, but cannot bring themselves to make the effort to diet. It's always tomorrow.

This attitude is very hard to shake off as long as there is a tomorrow. The discussion of motivation in Chapter 10 will show the remarkable changes that can occur when tomorrow will not do, when it has to be now.

Losing control

As I said before, the vast majority of panic attack sufferers, before treatment, believe that their attacks occur spontaneously and uncontrollably. They're unaware of exactly why they happen. They merely know that they tend to happen in certain situations and under certain conditions, so they avoid these as far as possible. They believe that once a panic starts, like an epileptic fit, they can do nothing but wait for it to run its course. This leaves sufferers with feelings of vulnerability and of having lost control of their lives.

It has been suggested that very dependent people are more liable to experience panic attacks. I have found no evidence to substantiate this in my work to date. It is true, however, that panic attack sufferers may, as a result of their panics, become very dependent. They may also grow to despise themselves because of this.

A woman who won't leave her home without her husband for fear of panicking has become very dependent on him. She may not have been a dependent person beforehand. Anne, described earlier, felt very resentful as a result of her dependency on her younger sister, who had done better than Anne at school and had a good job in a government department. She still lived at home with Anne and their widowed mother and was one of the few people with whom Anne felt safe to leave home. Anne felt angry with herself for her failure compared to her sister's success, as well as self-disgust because of her panics. She felt even more disgusted with herself that she had come to rely on her sister so much.

Naturally, once panic attack sufferers grow to hate themselves because of their panics and their dependency, this only serves to diminsh their efforts to overcome their disabilities. They believe themselves to be worthless and deserving of punishment. By perpetuating their attacks they are, in a sense, punishing themselves. Few panic attack sufferers are aware, initially at least, of this paradox, yet it is at the root of their trouble.

I have found that panic attack sufferers need to learn this, and that, on the whole, they like themselves better at the end of treatment than they did at the start. Their images of themselves come closer to their ideal. They're less negative towards themselves as people. They learn to like themselves a little.

Spasmodic panic attack sufferers will have noticed that their attacks are variable. Some days they will be able to face a particular situation, whereas on others that same situation might provoke greater anxiety and a possible panic attack. This is due to several factors.

The first of these is background anxiety. If sufferers have worries, their anxiety levels will be raised and they will be a step nearer to panicking than they would if they were calm. It then requires only a slightly increased concern that they might panic to set the panic attack spiral in motion.

People's susceptibility at any one time also depends upon their thoughts. If their thoughts and attention are absorbed by what they're doing, the idea that they might panic won't cross their minds. If, however, they have time on their hands, their minds wander to thoughts of panic. Alan, whose case was described in Chapter 6, used to worry about not having enough to do at work. He had noticed that he never panicked when he was busy. If he had no work, however, he would tend to feel very anxious and panicky. Several of the middle-aged women I have counselled also complained of feeling more panicky when they were bored.

Boredom and loss of identity

Middle-aged housewives are the main sufferers of agoraphobia. This isn't surprising in view of what we have learned of panic attacks so far.

In the first place this group is often subject to boredom. Women at home all day with labour-saving gadgets have plenty of time on their hands. Their children are at school, or grown up and leading their own lives. The women go shopping probably once a week to the supermarket by car. Unless they have a consuming interest or occupation, they tend to lose their sense of identity. They are wives and mothers, but on their own all day they feel they are neither. This realization can lead to feelings known as depersonalization, feelings that one has ceased to exist as a real, separate person. These feelings not unnaturally provoke anxiety.

When such people start experiencing panic attacks against this background of boredom and depersonalization, they retreat into their homes.

They are able to do so because they don't have to go out. They adapt their lives so that they don't have to face their panics. They don't leave the house alone. They become more dependent on the family and in doing so, paradoxically, they achieve some sort of identity. They are recognized as agoraphobics, whereas before they felt they were nobodies. They may remain housebound this way for years, lacking the motivation to change.

Agoraphobia in men is rare. But, as we have noted before, there is growing evidence that many men who become alcoholics are hiding their fear of panic attacks in drink. Walter, described in Chapter 6, tended to do this at the start of his panics. Most men have to continue with their jobs. Unlike housewives, they can't shut themselves away at home without it becoming obvious to everyone that there's something odd about them. Women who are not working, on the other hand, are able to do so unquestioned.

What sort of people are panic attack sufferers?

Overall, panic attack sufferers tend to disapprove of themselves and even to dislike themselves. This self-hostility, as it's called, tends to make them try less hard than they might to overcome their panics – they're always putting it off until tomorrow. In keeping with their often unconscious wish to punish themselves, they'll even feel panicky when enjoying themselves as well as when bored or insufficiently occupied. Whether acute or spasmodic panics develop depends upon the degree of general anxiety or worries that the individual has at the time.

What sort of sufferer are you?
A questionnaire follows to enable you to establish to what extent the characteristics I've just mentioned apply to you. It's important to remember that knowing yourself is a prerequisite to learning to handle yourself. I've often told people I've counselled that within the context of psychotherapy it's all right to fool others about yourself, that is, to pretend you're something you know you're not, but it's asking for trouble to fool yourself.

PERSONALITY QUESTIONNAIRE

This is designed to give you some idea of the areas of your character that might make you susceptible to panic attacks. Obviously, it's difficult to obtain a very accurate assessment of any one individual with a test as general as this. It is intended merely as a guideline, something to start you thinking. Try to answer the questions honestly.

1. You're looking forward to an evening out with your partner but your babysitter is taken ill at the last minute. Do you
   a Tell your partner to stay at home and go out yourself? ▨
   b Both stay home? ▨
   c Tell your partner to go alone and resignedly stay at home yourself? ▨

2. You're taking an important examination in a week's time and you've left your swotting too late so now you have to study full-time for the next seven days in order to stand any chance of passing. Friends call unexpectedly and invite you to go to the beach for a picnic with them. Do you
   a Decline the invitation, realizing it's your own fault you have to work so hard now? ▨
   b Throw caution to the wind and go, telling yourself you'll make up the work later? ▨
   c Go, but take some work with you and make sure everyone keeps the noise down so you can concentrate? ▨

3. You're at the supermarket checkout. You're only buying a couple of small items but you're already waiting behind two fully laden trolleys. Just as you've got to the front of the queue a young man rushes up with only one item and asks if he can go ahead of you, as otherwise he will miss his bus. Do you
   a Say 'no' and point out that you and all the others in the queue may be in just as much of a hurry as he is? ▨

    b Smile and say 'Please go ahead', admiring his nerve at asking? ▨

    c Relinquish your place to him politely, while inwardly seething at his cheek and lack of consideration? ▨

4. You've cooked a meal for four adults. Just as you're serving it an extra person turns up unexpectedly, having travelled some distance to visit you. Realizing there isn't enough food for five, do you

    a Say 'I'm sorry, I'd ask you to stay for the meal but there isn't enough to go round'? ▨

    b Warmly invite the new arrival to stay and give everyone smaller helpings, yourself included? ▨

    c Give up your portion, explaining that you're not eating anyway because you're on a strict diet? ▨

5. You're in hospital recovering from an emergency operation for appendicitis, which meant you missed a holiday abroad. Do you

    a Decide to make the most of your stay in hospital, catch up with some reading and make friends with the other patients? ▨

    b Look around at all the critically sick people and consider yourself very lucky your problem was minor and curable? ▨

    c Lie there thinking 'Why me?' and generally expect sympathy from nurses and visitors over your missed holiday? ▨

6. You win a raffle prize and select a box of milk chocolates. Back at your table another member of your party wins the last prize, a box of plain chocolates, and asks if you like plain chocolates. Not realizing why you're being asked, you reply that you do. In fact, you don't dislike plain chocolates but you prefer milk. The other person then asks you if you'd mind swapping your box of chocolates. Do you

a Refuse, saying that if you'd wanted plain chocolates you'd have picked them when you won your prize? ▨

b Swap boxes gladly since it was only a stroke of fate that you won them anyway? ▨

c Feel very annoyed but smile and agree to the swap? ▨

7. You have to buy a new outfit for an important interview. You take a friend shopping with you. You find an outfit that you like, but which isn't the sort of thing you usually wear. Your companion dislikes it because 'it isn't you'. Do you

a Trust your own judgment and buy it anyway? ▨

b Trust your friend's judgment and decide on something more like your usual style? ▨

c Buy it, but then have second thoughts when you get home and either change it or leave it in your wardrobe unworn? ▨

8. You're in a job that does not pay very well for the first couple of years. But once you qualify you'll be earning far more than all your friends. At present, however, your friends have much more money to spend on clothes and holidays than you. Do you

a Save up occasionally to buy or do something you want? ▨

b Do without, telling yourself you can wait – it's only two years after all? ▨

c Often feel fed up and resentful that you haven't got what they have? ▨

9. Your elderly mother is dying of an incurable illness. She wants to die at home so you have to help care for her. Do you

a Realize it will be a merciful release for her and try to make her last days as pleasant and cheerful as possible? ▨

b Keep thinking how much you'll miss her, how unfair life is and cry at her bedside? ▨

c Tell your other relatives you can't possibly help care for her as it upsets you too much? ▨

10. There's a repair that needs to be done in the house. You have to find a couple of spare hours to carry it out. Do you

    a Do it as soon as you can so that you can enjoy yourself and forget about it? ☐

    b Keep intending to do it next weekend and then forgetting, because there's always something interesting going on? ☐

    c Say you'll do it but keep providing yourself with all sorts of excuses not to, because you have no real intention of doing it at all? ☐

Yours answers

Now copy your answers into the boxes below making sure that you've ticked only one box for each question.

Looking after your own interests

Question		a	b	c
	1	☐	☐	☐
	3	☐	☐	☐
	4	☐	☐	☐
	6	☐	☐	☐

Mostly *a*s As a person who is quick to look after the interests of Number One, you are probably not a sufferer from panic attacks. Isn't it perhaps time you tried seeing things from someone else's point of view?

Mostly *b*s You seem to regard your rights as equally important or unimportant as those of others. If you do have panic attacks, you aren't likely to thwart your efforts to overcome them by your own dislike of yourself.

Mostly *c*s You appear outwardly considerate to others, but you don't match this with your inner feelings. Often you're only nice to people because you're too afraid to show what you really feel. The anger you feel unable to show others then ends up being directed against yourself. You are a panic attack sufferer in danger of spoiling your own progress by not regarding yourself as deserving to succeed. Try to be more honest in your feelings towards both yourself and others.

Positive thinking

Question		a	b	c
	5	☐	☐	☐
	8	☐	☐	☐
	9	☐	☐	☐
	10	☐	☐	☐

Mostly *a*s You seem to be able to look forward and get the best out of even the blackest situation. You should be able to overcome your panics without difficulty if you apply this attitude to them too.

Mostly *b*s You're tending to be positive but aren't completely successful. Consider the *a* answers and try to direct your way of looking at things more in that direction.

Mostly *c*s Re-read the alternative responses and consider changing your attitude to a more positive direction. There is nothing to be gained in life by wallowing in despair as you do. If you suffer from panic attacks you're unlikely to get very far until you try being a bit more hopeful.

Strong mindedness

Question		a	b	c
	2	▨	▨	▨
	7	▨	▨	▨
	10	▨	▨	▨

(Note: It isn't an error that question 10 appears twice in the scoring.)

Mostly *a*s You seem to know your own mind. That's not to say you're bossy or domineering. It means that you decide what you should do and stick to it. You should do well in overcoming your panics once you've decided how to go about it.

Mostly *b*s You tend to be a pleasure seeker. You decide to do something but allow yourself to change your mind if something tempting comes along. No doubt you often find yourself in trouble because, although you set out with good intentions, you probably never get things done when you should. This kind of behaviour isn't common in panic attack sufferers, unless they're also creating a great deal of anxiety for themselves by their failure to get things done on time.

Mostly cs You must learn to be more decisive. It's not wrong to take advice from someone, in fact it's a wise person who knows when to do this. But your problem is that even when you decide to seek advice you can't make up your mind whether or not to take it. You need to be much firmer with yourself. Try sticking to your decisions and this will help you overcome your panics. Indecision only provokes anxiety – and we all know where that can lead.

What sort of personality do you have?

These questions were designed to bring out your reactions to stressful situations. You may have responded in various ways, but overall you should be able to detect your usual behaviour patterns. People who scored mostly *a*s are those who take care of their own destiny and are unlikely to have panic attacks. Those scoring mostly *b*s are relaxed about letting others take their decisions for them, so they are unlikely to have panic attacks; those scoring mostly *c*s are frustrated at their own inability to express their real wants, which is usually a personality trait of people who have panic attacks. However, people scoring more in other groups may also be panic attack sufferers. You cannot put people into neat categories and expect them always to behave according to their labels.

9
ESCAPE

Panic attack sufferers, as I've said before, are afraid of panicking in public and making fools of themselves. If a panic starts in a public place, the natural reaction is to escape. Once sufferers think they are safe from public scrutiny, they relax because they're no longer under pressure to keep the panic under control. With the pressure removed, the fear of panicking vanishes, which, in turn, effectively halts the panic attack spiral. The attack fades away.

Knowing this, spasmodic sufferers can often cope by putting themselves in a position from which they can easily escape whenever panics may threaten. For instance, they sit in aisle seats in cinemas and theatres. They travel by car rather than on public transport. Corridor trains are usually less of a problem than buses because sufferers feel less confined and there is access to a lavatory as a refuge. Other sufferers have their own special forms of escape, which work so long as they believe in them, as was shown in the case of Jill and Martin, in Chapters 3 and 4 respectively.

Escape involves not only removing oneself from the situation, but also being able to give a plausible excuse for doing so. Panic attack sufferers tend to feel very silly and very reluctant to tell others about their problem. Frequently only the person closest to them, on whom they depend for support, will know exactly how they feel. Not surprisingly, even these confidants fail to understand the true nature of panic attacks. I say 'not surprisingly' because sufferers usually aren't able to fathom the reasons for the attacks themselves, let alone explain them to anyone else.

Sufferers may try to explain their predicament to relatives, but to a social gathering from which they have been obliged to make an abrupt exit, they will want to give an excuse rather than an explanation. This can cause problems if it happens frequently. To say always that you felt suddenly unwell begins to sound a little suspicious, as men who often have to leave pubs in a hurry have told me. Very occasional instances of feeling unwell arouse little interest in others; frequent instances of it do.

56

Countless excuses can be manufactured on the spur of the moment, such as dashing off to make sure you haven't left the car lights on. In fact, anything is better than saying, 'Excuse me, I'm having a panic attack. I'll just pop outside.' I have never encountered anybody who was as honest as this, at least not before treatment. Nevertheless, it might be a way of bringing an attack under control.

This brings me to an experience of my own. It happened when I was a student and changed my attitude to my spasmodic panic attacks.

Every two weeks we had to participate in a seminar. These seminars were attended by about a dozen students and a lecturer. We sat around a table in the department. The proceedings were relatively informal. One of the students would have prepared a short paper dealing with some aspect of our course. He or she then read this aloud to the rest of us. Afterwards we were supposed to discuss the views and opinions expressed. Although the discussion was unstructured and any one of us could speak as we wished, it was obvious that the lecturer expected each of us to make a contribution of some kind.

My problem was that I could never think of anything worth saying. If an idea came into my mind, I would carefully weigh it up and dismiss it as not being a worthwhile contribution.

If by chance I did decide that my comments were worth broadcasting, I would find that I had spent so long deliberating that the discussion had moved on and my point was no longer relevant. This left me time and again without having spoken in the seminar.

After several seminars of remaining silent I began to feel desperate. I knew the lecturer was not impressed by my failure to speak, yet I couldn't bring myself to blurt out what I regarded as any old rubbish (as I considered some others did). Finally, one week, I caught myself sitting there thinking 'What if I panic?' I decided I could always say I felt unwell and leave the room. But what if it happened again and again? I could hardly keep on using the same excuse. People would start getting suspicious.

Suddenly I realized that I was using my fear of a looming attack as an excuse to myself, so that I could get out of speaking in the seminar and remove myself from a situation in which I felt inadequate. Once I had realized that the danger of an attack was not real, but manufactured by me as a way out of my predicament, I no longer felt like panicking, even when I found nothing to say.

In my counselling, people have often told me that they have used the idea of an attack to get themselves out of something they didn't want to do.

Emotional panic

A feeling of being trapped, say in the middle of a row of seats at the cinema, can bring on a panic. But the trapped feeling can be emotional, as well as physical. Panic attacks can develop into an acute phase during marital breakdowns, when one party feels completely trapped with the other, and as if there's no way out of the marriage.

When Janice came to see me, she complained that arguments with her husband made her feel like this. Her previously spasmodic attacks had recently become acute. Her marriage was crumbling. She said that she hated being alone in the car with her husband because when he started arguing with her, she had no escape and would panic. Two other women I've counselled also expressed exasperation at their husbands' lack of understanding and intolerance of their conditions. One husband was enlightened as to the mechanics of panic attacks and his whole attitude to his wife's behaviour changed. She, in return, became much calmer and was able to start overcoming and controlling her panic attacks.

Why do you panic when you're enjoying yourself?

A recently devised theory known as Reversal Theory may provide an answer to this paradoxical question. Simply stated it goes: arousal in human beings is a continuum. At one end is low arousal, at the other is high arousal. Low arousal can take two forms, relaxation and boredom. High arousal can also take two forms, excitement and fear. Low arousal can either be pleasant (relaxation) or unpleasant (boredom). Likewise, high arousal in its pleasant form is excitement, and in its unpleasant form is fear. Reversal Theory proposes that some people (panic sufferers among them) tend to change suddenly from a pleasant to an unpleasant feeling. There is a thin line dividing excitement from fear, relaxation from boredom. Those panic attack sufferers who complain of panic spoiling their enjoyment are suddenly making this change, or reversal, from the pleasant to the unpleasant. The diagram opposite shows this.

It has also been suggested that certain groups of people see everything in negative terms rather than in positive ones, that is, they look on the black side all the time. Are panic attack sufferers guilty of this? We all know people who are said to enjoy a challenge. They revel in doing things the rest of us shy away from. They feel excitement, we feel fear. The arguments for radically changing our basic ways of thinking, of how we see world, are put forward in the last chapter of this book.

Be honest with yourself

Having examined the causes of the development of panic attacks and the characteristics of those most likely to experience them, you may already have gained greater insight into yourself, whether or not you have panic

REVERSAL THEORY

LOW AROUSAL .... HIGH AROUSAL	
Pleasant	
relaxation	excitement
Unpleasant	
boredom	fear

If the person thinks the situation is *pleasant* then
low arousal = relaxation
high arousal = excitement

If the person thinks the situation is *unpleasant* then
low arousal = boredom
high arousal = fear

Hence, by making ourselves see the situation differently
we can change the feelings we experience

Seeing the good side results in pleasant sensations
Seeing the bad side results in unpleasant ones

attacks. Before continuing with the next part of the book, which sets out ways of ceasing to be a victim, I urge you to think hard about the questions on pages 60–62 and to fill in answers where you can.

In order to gain control over your mind you must appreciate your lack of control so far. You must question your own motives and behaviour truthfully. Try not to deceive yourself. Your unconscious knows you best and it won't be fobbed off with excuses. If you're really serious about wanting to understand yourself better and cope with panics, then you will start to be honest with yourself.

If you feel you don't really care that much about your panics, I suggest that you put this book away until the day when you do. You won't succeed in gaining control of your own mind unless you are totally committed. It's no crime not to feel committed and there's no reason to feel guilty about it. Just let things take their course. You may find the commitment comes, as mine did, when you least expect it.

Your own case history : a questionnaire

When you visit a clinic and give your case history at the first interview, it provides the doctor or psychologist with basic background information and helps you to work out the sequence of your own trouble. Many people never really stop and think in detail about how their problems began until they are asked. Explaining their trouble to someone else often clarifies it in their own minds too.

Bearing in mind what you have discovered about panic attacks so far in this book, try to answer these questions about yourself honestly. Your answers will give you greater insight into yourself, and a record of your own case history for you to refer to at a later date should you wish to.

To simplify matters you can tick the box where appropriate. There is also space provided beside each box for you to add more information if you wish. Tick more than one box per question if relevant.

Today's date ....

1. **Try to recall the very first panic attack you remember having. Was it**
   less than a month ago ▦
   1–6 months ago ▦
   7–12 months ago ▦
   1–3 years ago ▦
   3–5 years ago ▦
   more than 5 years ago ▦

2. **Where did that first panic happen?**
   in a shop ▦
   at a social event ▦
   on public transport ▦
   in a place of worship ▦
   in the street ▦
   on holiday ▦
   somewhere else; where? ....

3. **Who was you with at the time?**
   a parent ☐
   a brother or sister ☐
   a friend ☐
   a child ☐
   no one ☐
   someone else; who?...........................

4. **How were you generally the day before the attack?**
   worried ▓
   unwell ▓
   pregnant ▓
   anxious ▓
   very tired ▓
   having premenstrual tension ▓
   something else; what?............................

5. **What happened when you panicked?**
   you left the place ▓
   you went home ▓
   you sat down somewhere ▓
   something else; what?............................

6. **What made you feel better?**
   leaving the scene ▓
   a drink of water ▓
   someone looking after you ▓
   a tranquillizer ▓
   something else; what?............................

7. **Did you avoid going into similar situations after this?**
   yes ▓
   no ▓
   If 'yes', what did you avoid?.....................
   ....

8. **If you answered 'yes' to question 7, for how long did you avoid that?**
   ....
   Do you still avoid it now? ▓

9. **If you answered 'no' to question 7, did you feel panicky next time you went back to the situation where you'd had the first panic?**
   yes ▓
   no ▓

10. **If you overcame that first phase of panics, do you have any idea how or why?**
    by avoiding the panic-provoking situation

for a while ▨

by speaking firmly to yourself ▨

no idea ▨

something else; what?..........................

11. When did your panics return?
less than a month ago ▨

1–2 months ago ▨

3–6 months ago ▨

longer ▨

12. When your panics returned, were you feeling anxious at the time about
a new baby ▨

marital problems ▨

employment ▨

your children ▨

something else; what?..........................

13. What did you do about your panics this time?
went to your family doctor ▨

ignored the panics and tried to carry on ▨

stayed at home ▨

something else; what?..........................

14. Why did you think your panics had returned?
due to a physical illness ▨

you were overtired ▨

no idea ▨

something else; what?..........................

15. Do you still think that that was the cause, in the light of what you've read here? If not, what do you now consider to be the cause? ....
....

16. What do you imagine those close to you think of your panics?
that you're mad ☐

that you should pull yourself together ☐

their attitude is understanding ☐

their attitude is sympathetic ☐

their attitude is impatient ☐

anything else? what? ....

PART II

Overcoming panic attacks

Now that we've looked at the general background to panic attacks, I shall go on to suggest positive and practical ways of overcoming them.

In our society there's a tradition of passive reaction to illness. If we break a leg, we go to hospital and lie there while it's re-set for us. We then do nothing but let nature and medicine take its course. We let doctors treat us, but we do very little, if anything, positive ourselves. Unfortunately, this traditionally passive role of the patient extends to mental illness too, and, particularly inappropriately, to the treatment of emotional problems.

Too many people with problems are unwilling to make any real effort towards self-help. They just want to take a few pills to make the depression or the anxiety, or whatever, go away. Although such medication has an important part to play, even in the treatment of panic attacks in the very severe acute phases, it is not a permanent answer.

It is important to remember that this book is aimed at helping everyone who has ever had panic attacks. It will also give greater understanding of the disorder to their nearest and dearest. Having said that, not all of the advice given in this book will be immediately suitable for all panic attack sufferers. If you were to receive personal therapy for your attacks, the treatment would be specifically tailored to your individual needs. Since this isn't possible in the case of a book, I urge you to follow my advice as to the steps you should or, more importantly, should not take.

Although a panic attack sufferer will find it very helpful to learn to laugh at the predicament, this is not compulsory! Nevertheless, the ability to do so does indicate a certain loosening of the tension surrounding panic attacks and can only be beneficial in the long term. Above all, you must be realistic in your approach, and not try to run before you can walk. Overall, the best advice in the context of progress in panic attack treatment is: if it feels right, do it.

10
FIRST STEPS:
THE FOUR PHASES

By now you should have identified the type of sufferer you are from the chart at the end of Chapter 6. There now follows a description of the symptoms characteristic of each of the two major phases (acute and spasmodic) and advice on the appropriate course to take. This depends upon the phase you are *currently* in, regardless of any phases you have been in in the past.

1 Acute phase

If you are currently experiencing the acute phase of panic attacks, your general level of anxiety is constantly high. You are always afraid, but don't really know of what. You can't settle or concentrate. You sleep poorly. You may even be afraid of being left alone and want someone with you all the time. There is usually a cause for such anxiety. In many cases it may be a recognizable event, such as a bereavement, or it may be less specific, the result of a longterm build-up of stress.

If your anxiety is overwhelming, you should seek professional help, initially from your family doctor. The advice for overcoming panic attacks on the next pages is not for you at this stage. First you must obtain relief for your anxiety state. After this, should you still find yourself experiencing panic attacks, then that is the time to read on.

In fact, even if your panic attacks stop once you have recovered from your excessive anxiety, it would be of great future benefit to read and understand the rest of this book. It's possible that you may have further panic attacks at some later date. Knowing in advance what to do about them will remove some of the anxiety from the situation should it arise.

2 Spasmodic phase

At certain times and in certain situations you might find yourself feeling panicky. Whether it happens frequently or infrequently, it can prove inconvenient if you are trying to make a good impression. If your attacks were frequent, you may have adapted and restricted your life so that you don't have to face panic-triggering situations at all. The greatest problem for sufferers of this kind is often a lack of sufficient motivation to change. As I have said already, overcoming panics isn't easy. It requires determination and effort. For many longterm spasmodic sufferers the degree of determination and effort required is too great. The choice is yours.

Motivation is the key to success
It would appear that success in overcoming panic attacks is equal to the desire to do so. The consequences of overcoming panic attacks have to be sufficiently good or important to make the effort worthwhile. Let us look at some examples of this taken from the experiences of people I've counselled.

Roger had rapidly developed an acute phase of panic attacks after feeling faint while returning home from work on the bus one summer day. He had been harbouring a lot of frustration and anxiety about his home environment. It was this that provided the high background anxiety for the acute phase.

Roger felt trapped in his marriage and, even more so, by his two-year-old son who pestered him constantly while he was at home. He kept trying to find something to keep the child amused, usually to no avail. If the child did, from time to time, leave his father alone, Roger was unable to relax because he was wondering how long it would last.

When his panic attacks began, Roger took to his bed, where he remained for three months. His doctor prescribed tranquillizers, but Roger made no real progress. Eventually he managed to return to work, but only because the family had found it impossible to manage on his sickness benefit. His employer had offered to pay for a taxi to take him to and from work, because he was still afraid to travel by bus. Financial motivation had finally got him out of the house. Later, when he came to see me, I advised him to try to put this problem into perspective. His son would soon grow up and lose interest in Roger's activities. Besides, it was not such a very long time after he returned from work that his son went to bed. Instead of trying to fend him off all the time, Roger should try deliberately to enjoy the child's company. This would help reduce the tension at home. Roger took my advice and said that it certainly helped. Before he had been constantly pushing such anxieties to one side instead of facing them. Finally the repressed anxiety had exposed itself in the form of panic attacks.

In Anne's case, desire overcame panic on one occasion.

Anne (Chapter 3) was afraid of most forms of transport except corridor trains (on good days) and cars. She did, however, have a passion for buying clothes. One day she had gone into town with her mother and sister. She wanted to visit a particular clothes shop towards the end of their trip and time was running out. There were no cabs around and the only way to reach this shop before catching the train home was by underground. Anne's desire to visit the shop was great enough on that particular day to allay her fear of panic on the underground. She was determined not to panic, and so she didn't.

Unfortunately such great degrees of motivation aren't present in most everyday situations sufferers have to face. I must also add that Anne's ability to overcome her panics that day on the underground didn't extend to her usual daily life, where change held less prospect of any substantial reward.

3 Acute-spasmodic

As I implied when addressing acute sufferers earlier in this chapter, it is quite common for an initially acute phase to settle down into a spasmodic phase once the high background anxiety has been resolved. In such cases the approach is the same as for the spadmodic-only sufferer. Nevertheless, it seems that acute-spasmodics may, for their pains, be more fortunate than the spasmodic-only sufferers. Since the former have known the extreme unpleasantness of the acute phase they often try much harder to rid themselves of panics completely. Spasmodic-only sufferers, on the other hand, often seem to lack such a fierce desire to overcome their symptoms totally.

4 Spasmodic-acute

Some sufferers undergo spasmodic attacks for years, and then they're suddenly catapulted into the acute phase by an emotional upheaval in their lives. The course to take in such cases is to treat the acute phase first and then to attempt to deal with any remaining tendency to panic, as described in the following chapters.

Remission – spontaneous or induced?

In a large percentage of cases panic attacks, even spasmodic ones, may go away seemingly of their own accord. The reason for this is usually that the sufferers forget about panicking in possibly threatening situations because their minds are engaged elsewhere. This does not mean, unfortunately, that the attacks are over for good. I have come across several cases where a sufferer has succumbed to panic during an emotional crisis after years unmarred by attacks. When it happens again, the victim tends to feel even more devastated, having thought he was cured.

Falling in love can cause panic attacks to go away – temporarily. Sufferers feel as if they're walking on clouds and are so engrossed in the object of their desire that they forget about their panic attacks. Falling in love also helps to make sufferers feel wanted and helps them forget the low opinion they hold of themselves. They feel they're special and don't deserve to panic, so they don't. Unfortunately, we can't fall in love to order! Loving someone like this needs to be reciprocated to produce the desired effect on the sufferer. Unrequited love may make sufferers even more miserable and enhance their dislike of themselves.

Anyone who has fallen into the way of responding to anxiety by panicking will always be able to panic in a threatening situation. But there is a choice. You can learn to control your tendency to panic if you make the effort. If you don't make the effort, panic will still lurk round the corner. It is highly unlikely, however, that having once learnt to control your panics, you will ever re-experience the dreadful acute phase again, whatever the provocation.

The outstanding case of one sufferer I counselled and the emotional upheavals that she withstood is a lesson to us all.

Paula was twenty-nine years old and married with two young daughters when she was referred to me after having overcome the acute phase of her panic attacks. Her acute phase had developed as a result of bereavement. In close succession, she lost her only brother, who died of cancer, and a very close friend, who suffered from a brain tumour. As she recovered from the bereavements, her attacks passed. Several years later she wrote to me.

'I overcame my panics completely,' she told me, 'and led a very normal life for two years. I then had a third child, but my husband resented the baby, as she disrupted the return of calm to his life; the other two girls were growing up and less trouble. He constantly complained of his commitments and said that if it weren't for the fact that I was financially dependent he would seek a divorce.

'I found a full-time job and employed a nanny. Initially my husband was very pleased and we went ahead with building an extension to our home, which we had been planning for years, the divorce forgotten. The extension proved a strain. Tempers were short and I was becoming increasingly worried. I was to have gone away on business but had a panic attack on the train, so I got off and didn't go. Things became progressively worse. By Christmas, after firing my second nanny, I suddenly broke down at the wheel of my car while collecting the children from school.

'I took two weeks off work to rest and went over all the "tricks" for coping with panics that I'd learnt from you. I overcame my fear and returned to work. My husband in the meantime became agitated at the prospect of my having another breakdown, and he attempted suicide. I had to give up my job and sometimes I thought I might fall apart. But I coped. I know I won't become very ill again; I feel I can cope. I also have the benefit of experience.'

These are the words of a very brave lady, and should be remembered when we other sufferers tend to become upset over the occasional spasmodic panic attack. Most of us have at least family or friends who help support us emotionally if we really do need it, even if they don't understand what we're going through. Paula had to fight. Her husband couldn't help her and she had no one else to lean on.

Self-reliance is vital
The quickest way to make a recovery is to take responsibility for yourself, and not rely on someone else to pick up the pieces. Learning to take control is vital in learning to cope with panics. I have already explained that because it is the sufferers' thoughts of panic in the first place that provoke the panic attack spiral, sufferers hold the key to their control, by controlling their thoughts. This is, however, easier said than done. But it can be achieved if the advice given here is followed.

The most common form of treatment offered for panic attacks – usually those diagnosed as agoraphobia – was, until very recently, some form of behaviour therapy, usually desensitization. For this treatment the sufferers were first asked, with the help of a therapist, to draw up a list of those places of which they were afraid. They then had to arrange the names in order, putting the least feared at the bottom and progressing to the most feared at the top. They were also given a course in progressive muscular relaxation, in which they were taught to relax the whole body systematically. They were then instructed to undergo what is termed *in vivo* exposure, usually accompanied by the therapist or a suitably trained nurse. This meant that they had to go to the least-feared place on their list. If they felt panicky, they were to remain there until they felt calm. They were to try to relax. They weren't encouraged to run away in the face of their fear. Gradually, at subsequent treatment sessions, they would progress up their list of feared places until they could finally go alone to the one at the top of the list.

This treatment was not only very time-consuming for the therapist as well as the sufferer, but it was found that all too often sufferers would relapse after having been left to their own devices for a while. The problem was that they never assumed responsibility for controlling their own panics. Throughout their treatment they were virtually told what to feel, and when, by the therapist. They came to believe they wouldn't panic provided they did what the therapist told them. Faith in a therapist in this instance was just as much of a false prop as taking a drink of water or a sip of brandy. If the sufferers had not become self-reliant, once away from the therapist they reverted to their old behaviour – panicking.

If you can follow the course of action outlined above, but relying on yourself and no one else, you will have achieved a great deal towards overcoming your attacks. If you can get yourself into a positive frame of mind and visit the feared places alone, you will make a great deal more progress than visiting them with a therapist or anyone else. Provided you rely solely on yourself, you'll always have all you need at hand when you have to cope with a crisis. If you learn to rely on someone else, you may find that person is not always there when most needed.

As a currently spasmodic sufferer, take heart. Once you are ready to start taking the initiative, to learn to harness the power of your own mind, you can only get better.

11
EDUCATION

My treatment programme is in three parts. The first of these is education. The rationale for this part is that, as I have said before, most people are at first convinced that their panics occur spontaneously and uncontrollably.

Spontaneity implies that sufferers have no influence over the onset of the panics. Although sufferers have usually realized that attacks occur in certain situations, they haven't noticed that panic happens only when they start to fear that it might. At this point I urge sufferers I treat to think very carefully of similar situations when panics have not occurred, and why they think this was so. Usually they remember instances but cannot produce reasons. I then describe the mechanics of panic attacks as I have described them in the first part of this book.

There is a great deal of information to digest and I repeat the essential points from time to time during the course of treatment. You, of course, are able to refer back to the earlier sections of this book as you need. I urge you to do this. There may be some important points you failed to notice the first time, or even the second or third time. Keep re-reading until you clearly and fully understand the reasons for your panics.

When you begin to take action to overcome your panics you will soon realize that the knowledge that they are created by you alone is vitally important. In some ways this realization is even more important than knowing how to control them. It gives you the power to control them and improve your way of life. When you know that the control is in your hands, one of the most feared aspects of panic attacks is removed, the fear aroused by never knowing where or when they might strike – the unpredictability.

I tell the people I counsel to monitor their thoughts closely when they are out, to try to catch themselves thinking, 'What if I panic now?' This thought will always be there somewhere in your head before you feel panicky. Sometimes it's unconscious and very fast, so that often you may not realize you've thought it until you find yourself beginning to feel afraid. With practice at watching for it you will increase your awareness of it. The greater this awareness, the better chance you'll have of stopping the fear, and the thought that leads to it. You stand no chance of stopping it if you're unaware of it in the first place.

Recognizing your vulnerability

Panic attacks cease to be unpredictable once you know what causes them. You will come to know when and where you are likely to be vulnerable. For example, if you're experiencing an unusually high degree of anxiety one day, you won't needlessly expose yourself to what you know to be a potentially panic-provoking situation. You will find that on some days you can face anything, anywhere; on other days you'll feel very vulnerable. The former occasions will gradually come to outweigh the latter as you learn that your vulnerability to panics is predictable.

Mothers naturally feel a higher degree of background anxiety if their children are ill. If you are prone to panicking and your child is ill, don't push yourself to face up to anything you feel might provoke an attack. This doesn't mean you should shut yourself away as soon as your background anxiety is raised. You should continue with your normal day-to-day life. Just be kind to yourself and don't expose yourself to any additional strain that could be postponed for a few days. If you find going to the dentist a nerve-racking experience and have an appointment at this time, you could spare yourself the ordeal until the child is better.

Learn to develop an awareness of your own anxiety levels and respond positively to them. This is not a licence to avoid doing things you don't want to do, but a way of controlling your anxiety – an approach I describe further in the next chapter.

Now that you know what is expected of you, we shall examine ways of achieving it. First, here is a summary of the points made in this chapter:

1. Keep re-reading the first part of this book to ensure you really understand what it says. Don't expect to take it all in at once.
2. Become aware of your initial panic-producing thoughts, for example, 'What if I panic now?' Watch for them. Make yourself aware of them.
3. Learn to predict your vulnerability to panic attacks.

Finally, give yourself some time to practise these points before continuing with the steps described in the following chapters.

12
COPING TECHNIQUES

The next part of the treatment is to acquaint yourself with the various techniques that can help you ward off a threatened panic attack. Forewarned is forearmed where panics are concerned. Again, the mere knowledge that you have weapons at your disposal to deal with your panics can itself help lessen the likelihood of an attack. To be sure that your methods of coping are reliable, you need to practise them on every possible occasion.

Read through the list of suggested techniques, and try to decide which methods you think would be suitable for you. Different variations work for different sufferers, and different techniques work in different situations. What's appropriate in one set of circumstances is not necessarily right for another. Above all, remember that there is no single correct solution for everyone. If you remain flexible in your approach and consider all possibilities for all situations before rejecting any, you will eventually find the techniques that are best for you. It may be that a subtle combination of different techniques works best. That's fine. Don't be afraid to experiment. Look upon this as an adventure of discovery.

Before describing the most helpful and desirable coping techniques I should like to get two of the most often used, but least desirable, out of the way: tranquillizers and alcohol.

Tranquillizers

Most panic attack sufferers who seek help from their family doctors will probably at some stage have been prescribed tranquillizers such as diazepam (Valium). These have varying effects on panics, depending how often you take them and exactly what you expect them to do. Tranquillizers do have a role to play in the treatment of panic attacks. For those experiencing very acute phases tranquillizers may provide a temporary respite from anxiety, without which life may be intolerable. So they are fairly important as a temporary measure. If tranquillizers are taken regularly, increasingly large doses are required. The body becomes addicted to them and withdrawal effects are experienced when they are missed. The withdrawal symptoms can mimic the original anxiety symptoms the pills were prescribed to alleviate and lead the takers to think they're still ill. In fact, the symptoms they experience are caused by overdependence on tranquillizers. If you have been taking tranquillizers daily for a long period and wish to give them up, you should ask your doctor how to go about weaning yourself off them.

At this point I must emphasize that if you have managed to cope without tranquillizers so far, then don't start taking them. Like smoking, it's better not to start in the first place than to try to give up afterwards (but please note that this advice is not directed to acute sufferers).

Although tranquillizers can be necessary for those who are suffering acutely, it is best to wean yourself off them as soon as you can, so that you can start practising positive techniques for coping with your panics. If you practise these techniques without tranquillizers, what you are doing will ultimately prove more beneficial.

Tranquillizers as a safeguard

It is often reassuring for the spasmodic sufferer to have a couple of tran quillizers handy in case of emergency. I carry a couple in my purse as a safeguard. I don't recommend taking them in anticipation of facing a potentially panic-provoking situation – that's cheating and merely serves to foster a dependency on tranquillizers.

I would only ever take a tranquillizer if I were suddenly, and totally unexpectedly, faced with a situation in which my anxiety might get completely out of hand. I should take one, for instance, if I were unlucky enough to witness a major road accident, or to get trapped in a lift. I would not, however, take a tranquillizer because I was travelling by car in case I saw an accident, or if I was about to use a lift and feared being trapped in it. I would recommend sufferers to carry tranquillizers for reassurance, but to resort to them only in a very unusual and frightening situation that arises totally unexpectedly, when to panic would cause a nuisance to others.

Alcohol and social drinking

Many people who become anxious and panicky in social situations turn to alcohol to calm their nerves. Usually alcohol is readily to hand at such functions. Social drinking to help you relax is not harmful in itself. Unfortunately, all too often it leads the sufferer to start drinking in anticipation of the event as well. Such behaviour can quickly lead to alcoholism. If you become abnormally anxious at most social gatherings, you should try to find out why and take steps to remedy the situation. Perhaps you are very shy, in which case it might help if you took a greater interest in others.

If you constantly attend social functions but really dislike them, you should seriously consider whether this is an essential or desirable way of life. If social situations are an unavoidable part of your life and the prospect of one makes you feel very anxious, then you might consider professional help.

One or two drinks can help you relax and enjoy an evening out, but alcohol is no longterm answer to panic attacks. Now for the more positive approaches to coping with panic.

Shoppers' relaxation

Many, if not most, panic attack sufferers have an aversion to shopping. It is particularly common among the men I have counselled. For these people I have devised a simple method of relaxing to help combat their anxiety. It isn't as totally and deeply relaxing as proper progressive muscular relaxation, but it is sufficiently relaxing to help arrest the panic attack spiral.

Imagine that you have just returned home after a long bout of Christmas shopping. You have walked a long way carrying heavy bags. Your feet and arms are aching. You sit down, put down the heavy bags, kick off your shoes and just relax in the chair. Let yourself go floppy as you feel the intense ache in your arms and feet ease – enjoy the release. That's all there is to it. There must be few readers who cannot imagine the physical aches and pains that follow such an expedition and the exquisite relief of that first sit down on returning home.

Now you see why it's called shoppers' relaxation. All you need to do is practise it in odd moments and in all sorts of places. Just picture yourself flopping into that chair and letting go. Do it now! If you practise in spare moments, on the bus, watching television, waiting in queues (you'll have to learn to do it standing up too), you will be able to do it very quickly.

Having practised it in normal situations, try it whenever you are feeling frustrated or annoyed, as well as when you feel panicky. It is not likely that shoppers' relaxation alone will prevent a panic attack. Nevertheless, it is a very potent technique when used in combination with one of the others I describe below.

Escape

Most panic attack sufferers use escape as a way of coping with their panics before they seek treatment. But escape is not always convenient and can make matters worse. Say, for example, your particular escape means you don't feel safe until you get home. Suppose you panic at work. You can't keep going home, time after time, without losing your job.

Two forms of escape are useful. One is potential escape, the other actual escape. Let us consider potential escape first.

Potential escape

As I have pointed out in earlier chapters, for many panic attack sufferers the knowledge that they can escape should they want to is sufficient to remove their fear of having a panic attack. You can provide yourself with a potential escape in circumstances where you think you may panic. Decide beforehand what you will do if you feel panicky.

If you are taking a seat in an audience, position yourself near the aisle. At one stage in my life I used to fear feeling panicky in church. I sat at the back of the congregation, yet not so separate as to draw attention to myself, and knew that I could leave if I wanted to. I never worried about what people would think. If you do something purposefully, others generally take little notice. If anyone did ask, I used to say that I had a cough and would need to leave if it got bad during the service. Then I would set myself goals. I would tell myself I would stay for just one more hymn. After that hymn, still feeling all right, I would extend the goal. Eventually I found that I had stayed for the entire service. That gave a great sense of achievement.

The secret is, having found your potential escape route, to break down what you have to do into easy stages, telling yourself that you can always leave at the end of any stage. Apart from this monitoring, try not to think about panicking but concentrate on what you are there for.

Actual escape

Actual escape is taking the routes you planned. If you take things in easy stages you may find you rarely have to use your escape route. But you mustn't be afraid to do so. If necessary, do escape in the earlier stages of a panic, go outside and compose yourself, then return. The most useful escape in many situations is the lavatory. Here you can shut yourself in and compose yourself unseen.

Try shoppers' relaxation to compose yourself, plus perhaps a few of the other techniques that I mention below. If you have come by car, you can slip out to the car park and sit there for a while.

Try to look upon escape as taking a breather, time in which to collect your thoughts before returning to the fray. Try not to take total escape and return home, but don't be afraid to do so if you absolutely must.

Whatever form of escape you use, use it deliberately. Don't leave things so late that you just rush out blindly. Don't let your panic attacks escalate to such a level before taking action. Before you escape, weigh up whether or not you can perhaps carry on a little longer, and each time you do this you will find your escape a little less urgent.

The question of escape from supermarkets bothers many sufferers. They believe that they can't leave until they've paid for the goods in their trolley.

This is not the case. If you really feel you must, there's no reason why you can't abandon a full trolley before you get to the checkout. I don't advocate your doing this too often, as the supermarket manager might take exception to your behaviour. Nevertheless, the option is there for you to use in an emergency. Often, merely telling yourself as you shop that you are free to leave if you wish is sufficient to give you confidence to continue and to keep panic at bay.

Positive thinking

This means adopting a positive attitude towards your panic attacks at all times. It means learning to laugh at yourself. You won't help yourself by taking a grim, pessimistic outlook, but you may help yourself by taking an optimistic one.

If you are trying to control your panic, but don't quite succeed, don't blame yourself for a failure – tell yourself what you did achieve. Each time people I counsel report their progress to me I point out to them the positive aspects of their behaviour, and gradually they tend to spot these themselves, instead of just seeing the negative side. Instead of saying 'I failed', they can say, 'I may not have succeeded totally, but it was good practice at coping.'

Keep telling yourself that you are progressing. It may not be sensational, or even remarkable, but always remember that it was the tortoise, not the hare, who finally won the race. Try to adopt this positive attitude towards your whole life. Never look back on an attempt at coping and pronounce it a failure. After all, you were brave enough to have exposed yourself to a potentially panic-provoking situation in the first place. You must have made some progress with your coping techniques, however slight. Next time, tell yourself, you will do better.

Naturally we all get our 'down' days, times when we feel like wallowing in self-pity. Do so if you must, but when you've had enough, dry your eyes and prepare to fight again. Remember that you owe it to those who care about you, and most of all, you owe it to yourself. Remember, too, that you're not the only person to have panic attacks. You certainly haven't had the worst ones; there's always someone who's gone one better. When things look black, take a deep breath, repeat to yourself, 'I shall win', and try again.

Not so long ago, during my own very acute phase of panic attacks, I can remember saying to my husband, 'There's one thing for sure, all this agony is not going to be wasted. I may be useless today, but I'll use all these experiences in my research', and I did. No experience need be written off as useless. It often takes a personal crisis of some kind to motivate people to achieve the best they can.

A new light on the situation

Positive thinking can also be used to take the fear out of those places where you feel most susceptible to panic attacks. Instead of letting your mind record them as frightening, start to see them in a new light.

We develop what is known as a mental set about places we know well. This means that once we become accustomed to a particular scene and have it fixed in our minds, we see only what we expect to see when we look at it. This holds true for people as well as places.

The road from my home to the town centre is travelled by me day after day. I think I know every single building and bump en route. In fact, sometimes I find myself at the traffic lights at the entrance to the town not being actively aware of having driven there. I have been engrossed in my thoughts. My surroundings have conformed to the picture of that journey that was held in my memory and therefore my conscious mind didn't bother with it.

This is what is known as mental set, seeing what we expect to see. Once we develop a mental set for a place we cease to see all its everyday facets. If, however, some quite large change had occurred, a building had been demolished for instance, it would have jarred on my mind and I would have become conscious of it.

A far more vivid instance to demonstrate the delusory power of mental set occurred to me recently. I took my seven-year-old daughter to spend the day with a friend, and then I went on to the local hypermarket to do some shopping.

While browsing through the frozen foods I heard children yelling, 'Mummy! Mummy!' I took no notice, didn't even look up. Then I felt a tugging at my sleeve. Puzzled, I looked down and even then it was some seconds before I recognized my own daughter and her friend. Being convinced she was elsewhere, I wasn't programmed to see her there, so I didn't, until she confronted me.

If you are a panic attack sufferer, the likelihood is that you have developed a mental set about certain situations or places. Let's take supermarkets as an example. You don't need to look around them, you think, to know that they're frightening places. I bet that if I asked you to imagine yourself in a supermarket, you'd picture yourself confused, hemmed in, amidst a crowd. But supermarkets aren't always like that. At times when they aren't very busy, they're airy and spacious. A customer can wheel a trolley freely up and down the aisles at great speed and even enjoy the feeling. You can stand back from the shelves and select your goods at leisure, unjostled.

Question the images you hold in your mind of the places you feel uneasy about. Try to visit them at their best and try to see their pleasant aspects. Afterwards, when you have to endure those places at their worst, you can recall the other, pleasanter image and keep that in your mind instead.

This takes practice, but is worth attempting. Try, too, really to look at your own surroundings, to see them as a stranger might and take in all the perspectives, rather than as someone who has become too accustomed to them to see everything.

Cognitive distraction

This ploy is most useful in a panic-provoking situation to divert your thoughts from a possible panic attack.

As I've often told people I counsel, panic attack sufferers are very egocentric, very vain. They concentrate on themselves, wondering if they will panic, rather than attending to the matter in hand. And they tend to imagine that everyone's eyes are on them and that people are going to stop and wonder why they're leaving the room. This is a big delusion. Other people are far too interested in what they're doing to worry about you.

If panic attack sufferers stop thinking about themselves and turn their attention to others for a change, they won't have time to think about panicking. For all you know, somewhere out there someone else has the same problem. See if you can tell who it is. You could go over and talk to that person. Make him or her feel at ease. This way you can train yourself to think of others instead of your panics and their many variations. If you are genuinely interested in someone else you will forget yourself and there will be no danger of panicking.

Sometimes you may find yourself surrounded by inanimate objects. It's not always easy then to centre your thoughts on others. Caroline had this problem. She hated walking home from work. In fact, she was afraid to do so for fear of panicking. Nevertheless, she bravely took my advice. I will relate it as she told it:

'It's a good walk home – a quarter of an hour – and what a terrible fight I had those first couple of months. I thought I would pass out or collapse on the pavement in a heap, but I didn't. I used your method of looking at homes, gardens and flowers. It did take a long time but I learned to relax and in the end I had no giddiness, no panic feelings. However bad you feel with the giddiness, just think about it, there is no pain! These thoughts I found very good on my long struggles home from work.'

A combination of positive thinking and cognitive distraction: Caroline was making a deliberate point of observing and commenting to herself on her surroundings as she walked. We usually fail to appreciate fully our everyday surroundings because we never really look at them. Try doing just that the next time you feel vulnerable. Ask yourself, 'Would I like those flowers in my garden?' 'Would I paint my front door that colour?'

One form of cognitive distraction is known as thought stopping. It means just what it says. In effect, as soon as you become aware that you are wondering whether or not you'll panic, stop and say to yourself, 'Don't be so stupid. It's all in my mind anyway.' I have also advocated to some people that they make this even more effective by wearing a fairly strong rubber band around one wrist. When they stop their thoughts they also tweak the rubber band. The discomfort incurred by the rubber band contracting against the wrist usually helps disturb any counter-productive train of thought.

Imaginal rehearsal

Imaginal is a specific term used in psychology. I refer to imaginal rehearsal here because it is useful for anyone practising these techniques to know the proper terms. This is a means of helping you prepare to face an anxiety-provoking situation that you cannot avoid. If you go through the situation in your mind beforehand, it will become more familiar and the happenings less unexpected, and therefore, less likely to provoke anxiety.

It is also useful to practise positive thinking while you imagine your situation. Tell yourself you will enjoy the new experience – go out to meet it as an adventure. If you are able to adopt this attitude you are well on the way to mastering your mind and ridding yourself of panics for good.

For the imaginal rehearsal, sit back comfortably in a chair. Practise the instantaneous shoppers' relaxation so that your limbs become heavy and you experience a pleasant sinking or floating feeling. Some people prefer to feel they are sinking down, while others would rather imagine that they are floating up. It doesn't matter which you do. Now slowly picture yourself in the situation that you are worried about. Keep telling yourself that although it's new it can't hurt you. You're in control. Work out any possible escape routes. Look at the situation positively. Picture the entire sequence of events as clearly as you can. Don't rush.

If you try to practise in this way several times before facing the situation itself, at the same time remaining as calm as possible, you might even come to look forward to it! A positive approach can work wonders.

These then are the coping techniques. You will have noticed that some are used to prepare yourself for situations, such as imaginal rehearsal. Some are used to forestall a panic when you are in a particular situation, such as cognitive distraction, positive thinking, and potential escape. Others serve to stop a panic, such as shoppers' relaxation (although this can be used to great advantage at any time), thought stopping and actual escape. You have to find your own most effective combination of these.

As long as you rely on doctors, relatives, alcohol or pills to make you better you won't make any longterm progress. There is no pill in the world that will take away panics for good and leave the sufferer fit to lead a normal life. In the final analysis the will to win must be yours. You must let your conscious will rule your unconscious actions. You must begin to take control. Don't let irrational fear creep up on you and overpower you. It will be a struggle at first, but in the end you'll win.

13
PRACTICE

The third, and very important, part of the treatment programme is to start putting your coping techniques into effect and begin going into situations that you have previously tended to avoid for fear of panicking.

The first step is to make a list of all these situations, ranging from those in which you feel merely uncomfortable, to those that you avoid totally. Begin by concentrating on the situation that offers the least threat to you. Once you have conquered your fear of that, work up the list, taking on bigger challenges each time. If there comes a time when you don't want to take on any more challenges, stop and reassess your position. Like Paul, you may find you have achieved all you really need to lead the kind of life you want.

Paul was forty-two years old and married. He hadn't been to work for over three years. He was an agoraphobic. He even used to feel tense and panicky when eating meals at home.

Over a period of months Paul was encouraged to practise various coping techniques. We began by working on his eating problem. With a combination of relaxation and positive thinking he overcame it. He used consciously to relax himself from time to time during mealtimes. This eventually became automatic. He got into the habit of thinking, 'Why am I afraid? It's only food. I don't have to eat it but I shall, because I want to.'

Having regained his confidence at mealtimes, Paul began to go to his local pub in the evenings. At first he told himself that he would go there just for five minutes, then leave. He could buy a drink if he wished, but he didn't have to drink it. While he was there he would make a conscious effort to relax, to concentrate on others rather than himself, and tell himself he was having a pleasant time. Paul gradually increased the amount of time he stayed. He decided how long he would stay beforehand, but could permit himself to stay longer when the time was up if he wished.

After a few months he was once again captain of the darts team, as he had been before his illness.

Paul then managed to go away on holiday with his wife. He also got used to taking his wife shopping by car, although he never went into shops with her. He had no desire to do so whatsoever. Whenever I mentioned that he might consider returning to work, Paul would have a slight relapse.

After three years Paul had lost any real desire to work. To go back to a job was a very big step that he just wasn't prepared to take. He didn't think he had anything to gain by returning to work. He had sufficient money. He already had a reputation in the neighbourhood for being ill 'with his nerves' so he didn't think he was likely to lose face any more than he already had by not going back. He had plenty of time now for tinkering with his car and for odd jobs around the house.

In the face of such total resistance there was little I could do. There may come a time when Paul feels he wants to take up the challenge and work again. If that happens, then he will be able to because he knows how to go about it. At present, however, he has no reason in the world to do so.

Paul had achieved all he wanted to lead a contented life. He had made enormous progress, and now he was content to draw the line. He stopped short of returning to work, just as Roger, in Chapter 10, stopped short of using the bus to go to work. With his employer offering him free transport in a taxi, Roger, not surprisingly, had come to prefer this mode of transport greatly and was quite happy to continue with it. There was certainly no motivation on his part to revert to going to work by bus, so he never mustered the courage to try.

When you make out your list, bear in mind how strongly you wish to do the things on it. It may be that, unlike Roger and Paul, your pride or self-respect spurs you on to overcome certain difficulties, even though to do so may leave you worse off in other ways. Self-respect has a large role to play in getting better. The more you have, the more progress you'll make.

When you have written your list, with the situations in order of difficulty, with the potentially easiest at the top, transfer it to the chart on page 86. This will help you to keep a record of your progress so that you can see how well you're doing. You are now going to expose yourself to each situation, working your way down your list and taking the items one by one. This may take you weeks, it may take months. It doesn't matter how long it takes, because you'll get there in the end.

You can approach it however you like. You can set yourself a specific time and day to expose yourself to a situation, or you can merely wait until you feel the urge to have a go. But be fair on yourself. Don't pick a day when you are under some sort of emotional strain or feeling under the weather. If, however, you find your plans constantly thwarted, ask yourself if your excuses are really as genuine as you're leading yourself to believe.

You may want to go over a situation in your mind – imaginal rehearsal – a few times before you try it for real. You may want to face up to difficulties gradually, or you may prefer to throw yourself in at the deep end.

Getting used to supermarkets
If you're afraid of going shopping at the supermarket you could approach it in the following way. Go there with someone. Get your friend to wait outside while you walk round the shop with an empty wire basket, buying nothing. You know you can leave the shop at any time, but you're not going to think about that once you're inside. You're going to try to concentrate on other people and the goods on the shelves. Make sure you don't have any shopping bag with you and that you replace the basket before leaving the shop. (We don't want anyone arrested for accidental shoplifting.) The first time you try this spend about five minutes in the shop, just walking round. Gradually increase the time until you find it no effort at all to wander round. Then start to buy a few things. You will find your confidence grows very quickly after the first few times.

You might prefer to practise going round the shops when they are at their least crowded, gradually working your way towards the busier times. Always remember that should you want to leave a shop before paying and get anxious waiting in the queue at the checkout, you have only to leave your wire basket, or trolley, and walk out.

If one day you do feel a little panicky in the shop, don't worry. It's not the end of the world. It's just an opportunity to practise your coping techniques. Think positively!

Getting used to buses
A similar sequence could be useful to someone who disliked travelling by bus. To begin with you could just practise standing at the bus stop until the bus comes, but not getting on. Pretend you're waiting to meet someone off the bus if you feel conspicuous. When you feel happy about just waiting for the bus, get on it and get off at the next stop. You may prefer to choose a time when the bus is likely to be fairly empty to practise first. As you sit on the bus try cognitive distraction. Look out of the window, listen to people's conversation, marvel at how well you're doing. Relax and enjoy the ride. With practice this will become second nature. As you gain confidence you can increase the number of stops you travel.

Be persistent
Almost any everyday situation can be faced by breaking it down into easy stages. Keep telling yourself as you practise that you're in control and

there's nothing to be afraid of. Keep making yourself go floppy, using shoppers' relaxation, and try to enjoy what you're doing. You can't panic unless you let it happen.

Now I have advised you to progress gradually down your list. Nevertheless, if one day you wake up with a very strong desire to do something way down your list, then do it. Don't be over-cautious. If you really want to do it, you can.

Practice is bound to be beneficial, whatever form it takes. You will never fail. You may not succeed totally every time, but progress will always be made, experience gained. You will have managed something each time, however little. Keep a note of exactly what this was.

Don't let anyone else tell you how and when you practise. Don't let anyone else criticize your performance. It's for you alone to decide what you practise and when, and you alone can judge your achievement. After all, your inner thoughts are more important than your observable actions. How can anyone else possibly know what your thoughts were and how well you were controlling them? For instance, you may have stayed in the supermarket for five minutes, but only you will know whether you were obsessed with a fear of panicking and ready to run, or just looking at the merchandise, wondering what would make a tasty meal and comparing prices.

PROGRESS CHART

- List here all the things you want to achieve, the easiest first, progressing down to the hardest. Make your list as long as is practicable; you don't have to fill up the entire chart unless you need to.

- There is space to record up to five attempts at each item. Again, make only as many attempts at each as you wish. Move on when you're ready.

- Don't make the jumps between items too big. For instance, don't follow 'Walking to the garden gate and back' at No. 1 with 'Going shopping alone' at No. 2. That's too big a jump. You need to put more stages in between.

- Remember to record all positive aspects of each attempt.

- Extend your list on a separate sheet of paper if you wish.

Task	Attempt	Date done	Comments
1.	i		
	ii		
	iii		
	iv		
	v		
2.	i		
	ii		
	iii		
	iv		
	v		
3.	i		
	ii		
	iii		
	iv		
	v		
4.	i		
	ii		
	iii		
	iv		
	v		
5.	i		
	ii		
	iii		
	iv		
	v		

14
STAYING PANIC-FREE

This chapter is about how you can avoid succumbing to any further phases of panic attacks in the future. As I have already explained, once you have learned how to panic you will always be able to, unless you take very positive steps against it.

After you have conquered your panic attacks, and feel they are gone for good, there may still come a time when you suffer one unexpectedly, perhaps while you are under emotional strain or unwell. If this happens, take whatever action you consider to be appropriate or necessary at the time. Afterwards you should regard the incident as a minor lapse. It need not be the start of a further phase of panic attacks. Look at it positively as an opportunity to show you're still in control.

To worry about a small lapse like this would be very unproductive. Indeed, worry is a luxury you must give up in order to safeguard against panic attacks. To worry is detrimental to health, it's a form of stress. Try to use any anxiety you feel productively. Someone anxious about passing an exam can turn anxiety into positive energy and use it to study better. The right degree of anxiety, as I said earlier, can make you give your best performance.

It's no good worrying about something you can do nothing to change. Take the case of the parent who worries that a child will fail its exams; or the case of the child who's worrying about the results. Both are worrying unnecessarily. Neither can change the outcome of events by worrying. No amount of worrying on the parent's part can make the child learn its work better; in fact, the parent's concern may be interpreted as nagging and make the child stop working altogether.

In spite of the futility of this kind of worry, society expects it of us and tends to make us feel guilty for not indulging in it. Recently, my teenaged son asked me if I was worried about his awaited exam results. He was horrified when I said, 'No'. I pointed out that it wasn't that I didn't care. I'd like him to do well. On the other hand, because I couldn't possibly influence the outcome by worrying, the only thing my worrying might achieve would be my ill health, and I didn't see the point in that.

Worry has a place if you can take steps to change the circumstances that cause it. If you are anxious and it's in your power to change things, you can use your anxiety positively. If you can't change things, stop worrying. It's easier each time you do it. I came across a rhyme recently that sums up exactly what I have just been trying to convey:

> For every evil under the sun
> There is a remedy or there is none
> If there be one, try to find it,
> If there be none, never mind it!

Reversal theory

I introduced reversal theory in Chapter 9. This too is something of which you should become aware.

If you have a tendency to regard relaxation as boring, or if you become afraid, rather than excited, at the prospect of anything new, try thinking the opposite. It's the way we label our feelings that influences us rather than the feelings themselves.

Many years ago I discovered this on a fairground ride. I went on a roller-coaster for a dare, although I was scared. As I sat there waiting for it to start, I felt myself tensing up. My stomach muscles especially were tense. I decided to look upon the ride as a pleasure. I deliberately relaxed my muscles and, as the ride began, I let myself go with it instead of tensing up and trying to resist it. I found it very pleasurable.

If you tell yourself that something is exciting, you will probably feel excited. If you believe something to be frightening, you will notice only all the bad points about it. Try it for yourself. The next time you feel apprehensive about doing something, look upon it as an exciting adventure. After all, you're going to go through with it anyway. The only difference will be whether or not you enjoy it.

Once you learn to harness the power of your mind in this way you will be able to control your life far better. You can allow yourself to feel either positive or negative about almost anything. Why not try the positive more often?

A sense of identity

Panic attack sufferers who depend on others for long periods may, as a result, lose a sense of their own identities. To have self-respect, a sense of your own worth and your value to others, you must be sure yourself who you are. It isn't enough just to see yourself as someone's parent or someone's spouse. What happens if your spouse dies or your children marry and move away? You lose your identity.

Finding yourself need not be traumatic or upsetting. It's merely a case of acknowledging the person who has been inside you all along. The better you know yourself, the easier it becomes to make the right decisions in your life. Many of us go too far through our lives having been led to believe we are one thing, yet constantly feeling thwarted and frustrated because we are really something else.

People who have known us the longest are often the least ready to alter the images they hold of us, to update them. They don't readily accept changes in us, but go on seeing us as they did in the old days and expect us to behave accordingly. You too may be guilty of this attitude towards others. Do you still see your children as the same people they were when they were young? What about your brothers and sisters, how do you see them? We tend to create our own images of those important to us and then expect those people to behave consistently with our images.

As you change and grow, it is difficult to get other people to acknowledge the new you. The only way to do it is to be true to yourself in the way you behave towards them. Eventually, they will accept you as you are. Chapter 19 describes simple ways in which you can begin to explore your own potential. Proceed now if you feel confident but if the idea scares you in any way, leave well alone. The time is not right. Consider it again perhaps in a few months.

15
LIVING WITH STRESS

Most of us do not fully realize the stressful nature of many normal events in our lives. In 1967 two researchers, T. H. Holmes and R. H. Rahe, drew up a list of common life events that cause stress and rated each one on a scale of 1 to 100. Their research showed that people who scored 300 or more within a six-month period or less were in danger of suffering a major illness as a result. Over 150 points gave a 50 per cent chance of stress-induced illness, whereas a score of less than 150 reduced this possibility to less than 33 per cent. Therefore, the higher a person's score, the greater the need to take steps to reduce stress.

Here are examples of stressful life events and their scores:

Death of a spouse	100
Retirement	45
Change in number of marital arguments	35
Change in sleeping habits	16
Holiday	13
Christmas	12

The stress in each situation is caused by the need to adjust to change; the greater the adjustment required, the higher the stress factor. Although most of us would expect to feel stressed at the death of a spouse, divorce or the loss of a job, there are many situations generally regarded as pleasurable that also produce stress. The most notable of these probably are going on holiday and retirement.

Large numbers of people plan and book their annual holiday in eager anticipation, only to find in the event, if they are honest, that they'd have had a far more relaxing time at home. Why?

Several factors may play a part. A family includes individuals of varying ages and interests, and the more children there are, the more variety there may be. Going on holiday, these indivduals uproot themselves from familiar surroundings and routines, and are thrown into closer proximity to one another for longer periods of time than they usually have to endure at home, where they each have separate patterns of daily life. It is not surprising that petty squabbles arise.

In addition, going away on holiday may involve making reservations, deciding what to pack, worrying about missing the train or aeroplane and, for those people who do not enjoy travel, the journey itself. In order not to ruin everyone else's enjoyment of the holiday, however, people may suppress their true feelings and pretend they are having a good time.

Many people eagerly look forward to retirement, to getting out of the rat race and enjoying their leisure. But not everyone is really prepared for the change in lifestyle. There may, of course, be a change in the level of income, but there also is a loss of structure to the day and contact with people outside the home. People often feel a loss of identity when they no longer have a job to do, particularly if they do not have other activities to occupy them. At this time, many people sell their family home and move to what they have dreamed of as their ideal retirement in the country or on the coast, and in doing so they bring on themselves even more radical changes and may suffer from anxiety or depression. The change in lifestyle brought by retirement alone is great and needs time for adjustment without the added worry of having to cope simultaneously in a totally new environment.

Human beings are creatures of habit at heart. We need familiarity in some areas of our everyday lives to lend stability. Familiar situations and relationships do not require a great deal of watchfulness because we can reliably predict what is going to happen next. They do not tax that part of our brains that analyses new situations and puts us on guard for the unexpected or the unknown. When we know what to expect of a situation we can relax.

We usually are well able to cope with changes in parts of our daily routine or environment, but to try to cope with too many changes may put too great a strain on the warning system and create anxiety. Therefore, it is best to change your life one step at a time. For example, given the choice, it would be ideal to move house, yet still live with the same people, or to change jobs yet keep the same living companions and environment. Of course, circumstances are not always ideal, and often people have to move home to take a new job. Although this might be accompanied by very positive feelings, such major changes to our lives also cause stress.

People differ as to how much change they can cope with at one time. Anxiety-prone people need to take change in small doses. Others, with what's termed a low arousal threshold, can cope with far more change before they become uneasy. Such people are often seen living rather precarious lives of their own choosing simply because this is what is required to 'turn them on'.

Situations where the outcome cannot reliably be predicted – such as not knowing whether you will pass an important examination or being made redundant and not knowing when, or if, you'll find another job – provoke anxiety. The best response to such situations is to take each possible outcome in turn, write it on a piece of paper, and then work out exactly what you'd do in the event of each outcome.

In this way you are doing something positive, taking your destiny into your own hands even though your future is uncertain. It is the belief that you are unable to control the future that provokes depression and anxiety. Doing something, however hypothetical, can allay this sense of helplessness as well as prepare you to act when the time comes.

Although the advice offered so far has been directed specifically at panic attack sufferers and those close to them, the following suggestions will help everyone to cope more effectively with the everyday stresses of life. It is important to approach these procedures with a positive outlook. They are to be enjoyed. They are non-competitive and are not for striving over, as that would only turn these stress-reducers into stress-inducers. By making a few alterations to their routines, panic attack sufferers and non-sufferers alike can improve the quality of their lives.

Deep relaxation

In recent years large numbers of patients referred for psychiatric treatment for anxiety-related disorders have been given a course of relaxation training. This is a very beneficial exercise for panic attack sufferers and non-sufferers alike to practise regularly.

The ability to allow the mind and body to relax completely is something that does not come automatically to members of our highly stressed society. It must be learned and practised. Paradoxically, the very people who would obtain most benefit from it – the harassed, the overworked – are those who claim to be unable to find the time to practise it.

All too often time spent truly relaxing is equated with time wasted. This is not so. Time spent acquiring the skill of relaxation is repaid many times over in greater mental efficiency and enthusiasm for life.

It is not possible to practise deep relaxation effectively while reading a book. In order to overcome this obstacle, I suggest that to begin with you merely read and re-read this chapter until you fully understand what is involved.

Ideally, the next step is to tape-record yourself, or someone whose voice you find soothing, reading the relaxation instructions (pages 94–8) slowly, softly and clearly. Then you can practise while listening to the tape.

If you do not have access to a cassette recorder, you will have to do the best you can by reading the instructions until you know them well enough to practise from memory. Although this is not a very effective method for a beginner, once you have learned to relax, you can use it easily.

Another possible alternative to using a tape recorder is to ask someone to read the instructions aloud to you as you relax. The success of this method depends upon the competence of your reader, whether he or she is able to read the instructions slowly enough and in such a way that you are able to forget the reader's presence in the room with you and concentrate solely on the instructions.

Pre-recorded relaxation tapes with suitably soothing voices are produced commercially, and can be very effective.

Preparations

You must set aside at least ten minutes for yourself daily. A little frequent practice is more beneficial than longer, less frequent periods. I have often been told by people that they wanted to practise but were prevented from doing so by interruptions of various kinds. This is an excuse. There are certainly some people who, perhaps as a result of bad housing or of being single parents of small, very active children, do not seem to have such an opportunity. However, the majority of us can, if we have the will, find a mere ten minutes in an entire day in which to practise. Even if you share with others who may be disturbed, this is possible. You can listen to your tape through headphones – maybe while lying in bed at night.

When you have chosen your ten minute period, make sure that the other occupants of your home know they are not to disturb you unless there is a dire emergency – nothing less than a threat to life or limb. If you are totally unable to assert yourself in such a way, you have already found one major cause of your anxiety and tension.

Mothers of small children should take the opportunity to practise while their children are asleep. Exhaustion at the end of the day is no excuse – in fact, it indicates a good time for relaxation. You can't be too exhausted to relax.

Bedtime is often a very suitable time for beginners to undergo relaxation training, especially for those who have difficulty getting to sleep. In bed one is usually warm yet unencumbered by restrictive clothing. Many people report falling asleep in the course of a relaxation practice, and that is no bad thing.

If you decide to practise at some other time of the day, choose a comfortably warm place where you feel at ease. Take the telephone off the hook – it's only for ten minutes after all. If you have neighbours who are in the habit of dropping in for a visit without warning, let them know beforehand the time when you will be relaxing so that they aren't offended or worried when you don't reply to their call.

Having taken all possible precautions to ensure an uninterrupted ten minutes, you are ready to begin. Although you will seek to practise undisturbed at first, once you have become really proficient you should be able to shut out the outside world and relax almost anywhere. However, this does take time.

Now lie down comfortably on your back, either flat or with your head and shoulders propped up on cushions or pillows. The position you choose is not important provided you feel comfortable in it and able to carry out the relaxation instructions as described.

In the instructions below, the words printed in *italic* are the ones to be recorded for the relaxation training session. Additional instructions and explanations are printed in regular type and are not to be recorded. After each instruction there is a set of six dots to indicate a pause while you carry out the spoken instruction. I cannot specify the length of the pause because it will vary from person to person. Before you make your tape, you must find your optimum length of time. To do this practise reading the instructions aloud while attempting to carry them out, and time yourself.

Instructions

Lie back comfortably . . . . . .
Slowly take a deep breath in through your nose, counting silently to three
    as you do so, watching your chest and then your stomach rise as the air
    fills them . . . . . .
Hold the breath for a moment . . . . . .
Exhale slowly through your nose and mouth, counting silently to three
    . . . . . .

It is important not to 'overbreathe', that is, to inhale more than you exhale. This can result in an imbalance of oxygen in your system and cause you to feel light-headed or dizzy. As you tape this, therefore, breathe as instructed so you know how long the pauses should be.

Now repeat the process
Breath in, slowly . . . . . . and breathe out . . . . . .
Your eyes may now feel as if they wish to close. Let the lids become heavy
    and close . . . . . .
Breathe in slowly . . . . . . and out . . . . . .
In . . . . . . and out . . . . . . In . . . . . . and out . . . . . .
Once more, in . . . . . . and out . . . . . .
Continue breathing normally.
Focus your attention on your left foot
Wiggle the toes of the left foot . . . . . .
Now tense all the muscles in your left foot, pull them as tight as

you can . . . . . . Imagine them knotted together, really tight . . . . . .
Hold it . . . . . .

If you tend to get cramp just tense the muscles momentarily and not too hard.

Now release the muscles in your foot, spread out your toes and feel them
loosen . . . . . . feel your instep loosen . . . . . . feel it grow heavier . . . . . .
feel it sink down, down, down . . . . . . Now focus your attention on the
calf muscles in your left leg . . . . . . Tense these, pull them as tight as you
can . . . . . . imagine them knotted together, really tight . . . . . .

Again, be careful not to tense too tight or too long if you tend to get cramp.

Now release the calf muscles . . . . . . feel them unwind, become free . . . . . .
feel the lower half of your leg grow loose and heavy . . . . . . Feel it sink
down, heavy as lead . . . . . .
Now concentrate on the thigh muscles of your left leg . . . . . . Tense them
. . . . . . feel them tighten up and knot . . . . . . really tight . . . . . . Now
release them, let them go loose and slack . . . . . . Feel them melt as your
entire left leg and foot become relaxed and heavy . . . . . . Feel it becom-
ing heavier, heavy as lead . . . . . . Feel it sinking . . . . . . Sinking down,
down, down . . . . . .

As you proceed, don't worry if parts that you've already relaxed begin to tighten again – for example, if you inadvertently tense your calf muscles again while working on the thigh. These areas will relax again when you complete work on the area of the body in question.

Some people find it more comfortable and effective to substitute 'light as air' for 'heavy as lead' and 'floating' for 'sinking'. Try this if the heavy feeling eludes you.

Next focus your attention on your right foot. Wiggle the toes of your right
foot. Tighten all the muscles in your right foot . . . . . . your toes, instep
. . . . . . imagine them knotted together, really tight . . . . . . Hold it
. . . . . . Now release the muscles in your foot, spread out your toes, and
feel them loosen . . . . . . feel your instep loosen . . . . . . feel your foot
become smoothed and heavy . . . . . . feel it yet heavier . . . . . . relaxed
and heavy . . . . . . feel it sink down, down, down . . . . . .
Concentrate on the calf muscles in your right leg . . . . . . Tighten them
. . . . . . Hold it . . . . . . Now release the muscles . . . . . . feel them
unwind, become free . . . . . . feel the lower half of the leg grow loose and
heavy . . . . . . feel it sink down, heavy as lead . . . . . .

Now the right thigh. Pull the muscles really tight . . . . . . tight as you can, and hold . . . . . . Slowly release the muscles . . . . . . feel them unwind and loosen . . . . . . feel them melt as your whole right leg becomes relaxed and heavy . . . . . . Feel it becoming heavier, heavy as lead . . . . . . Feel it sinking . . . . . . sinking down, down, down . . . . . .

With practice, by this stage you may experience the sensation that you have no legs at all. This feeling is a releasing of tension and an indication of success, so do not become wary or afraid. Enjoy the sensation; be positive about it. These feelings can do you no harm in themselves so allow yourself to go along with them.

Now concentrate on your left hand. Wriggle your fingers, then make a fist . . . . . . Clench it tight, tight as you can . . . . . . squeeze it . . . . . . Now release your fist, let your hand fall open and loosen . . . . . . feel it become limp and slack . . . . . . feel it grow heavy . . . . . . relaxed and heavier . . . . . . feel it sink down, down, down . . . . . .

Now think about your left forearm . . . . . . tense the muscles . . . . . . tight as you can . . . . . . Now let them go . . . . . . feel them unwind, become free . . . . . . loose and limp . . . . . . feel your forearm sink down, hang heavy as lead . . . . . .

Move on to the upper arm . . . . . . Pull the muscles tight, tight as you can . . . . . . Hold it . . . . . . Release your upper arm . . . . . . feel the tension melt away . . . . . . Feel your whole left arm grow loose and relaxed . . . . . . feel it become heavy and sink down . . . . . . as it sinks it becomes heavier, heavy as lead . . . . . .

Next the right arm . . . . . . Wriggle the fingers of your right hand, then make a fist . . . . . . Clench it tight, tight as you can . . . . . . Squeeze it . . . . . . Now release your fist . . . . . . let your hand fall open and loosen . . . . . . feel it become limp and slack . . . . . . feel it growing heavy . . . . . . relaxed and heavier . . . . . . feel it sink down, down, down . . . . . .

Tighten the muscles in your forearm . . . . . . hard as you can . . . . . . Now let them go . . . . . . feel them unwind, become free . . . . . . let your lower arm and hand grow loose and limp . . . . . . feel it sink down, heavy as lead . . . . . .

Now move on to the upper arm . . . . . . Pull the muscles tight, tight as you can . . . . . . Hold it . . . . . . Release your upper arm . . . . . . feel the tension melt . . . . . . Feel the whole right arm grow loose and relaxed . . . . . . Feel it become heavy and sink down . . . . . . as it sinks it becomes heavier, heavy as lead . . . . . .

Now both your arms are sinking down, loose and heavy . . . . . . heavy as lead.

If you are fortunate, you will by this stage have become unaware of both your arms and your legs. Do not, however, become impatient if this sensation eludes you for now. Keep practising and it will come, perhaps only momentarily at first.

Your limbs have now drifted off into a soft, relaxed state. Only your torso and head remain . . . . . .
Tighten the muscles in your stomach and buttocks . . . . . . Pull really hard . . . . . . Hold it . . . . . . Now let go . . . . . . Feel the muscles loosen . . . . . . Feel them soften and melt . . . . . . Feel them spread . . . . . .
Now tighten the muscles in your chest, shoulders and back . . . . . . squeeze them as tight as you can . . . . . . Hold it . . . . . . Now let them go . . . . . . Feel your whole body soften and spread . . . . . . Feel it loosen . . . . . . Feel it grow heavy . . . . . . heavier . . . . . . Feel your body sinking down . . . . . . heavy as lead . . . . . .
You are submerged up to your neck in a warm bath . . . . . . You can feel nothing at all below the water . . . . . . just warm and relaxed.

If the thought of yourself up to your neck in water bothers you, alter the wording so that instead you imagine your body sinking into a pile of feathers, perhaps, or warm sand, leaving your head exposed.

Now frown . . . . . . hard . . . . . . Clench your teeth . . . . . . tight as you can . . . . . . Feel the tension in the back of your head, your face . . . . . .
Now let go . . . . . . feel the lines on your face ironed out . . . . . . let them become smooth . . . . . . unclench your teeth, relax your jaw . . . . . . Breathe in slowly . . . . . . and breathe out . . . . . . rhythmically . . . . . . Feel the totally relaxed, heavy sensation all through your body . . . . . .
You feel completely relaxed . . . . . .
Enjoy the heavy, sleepy feeling . . . . . .
Feel a pleasant sensation of warmth washing over you as if you're resting on a sunny beach . . . . . . Feel a light breeze cooling you and listen to the waves . . . . . . the waves build up as you breathe in . . . . . . and break on the shore as you breath out . . . . . .
Lie there, relaxing for a while

At this point leave the tape blank for about thirty seconds. The slight noise caused by playing a blank tape will enhance the image of waves breaking on a beach.

If a warm, sunny beach is not an idyllic setting for you, substitute one that is. For instance, you might prefer floating on an air bed, sitting beside a lake, fishing or lying in the bath. We each have a favourite place where we can forget our everyday cares and mentally drift for a while, untouched by the real world.

Now you have rested......in a moment you will wake up......I shall count slowly to five. As I count you will gradually feel more and more awake. On the count of five you will be fully awake again and feel refreshed......
One......Two......Three......Four......Five......

Switch off the tape recorder.

Do not try to get up immediately. Sit up gradually. You may feel a little light-headed immediately afterwards, but the sensation won't last long. Try to enjoy it; don't run away from it.

There are, of course, many variations on the relaxation exercise, but the basic principles are the same:

1. Relax the muscles of the body. Tensing and releasing the various parts of the body in turn helps to make you aware of any hitherto unnoticed tension there.
2. The process of tensing and releasing the different areas of the body also serves to focus your attention on the matter in hand. Some people report lapses of concentration; they find themselves drifting off and thinking of other things. If you find this happening to you, just continue with the relaxation procedure from the point at which you find yourself. As you become more competent you will be able to relax the body more easily and in a shorter time.
3. Once in a state of physical relaxation, let your mind dwell on a setting that promotes a sense of calm and well-being for as long as you wish.

I have a tape of the sound of the sea that helps this third stage. I also have one of country sounds and another of soft 'magical' music (see page 124). For me, all of these enhance the sense of relaxation in the third phase.

Never underestimate the power of your mind. You will be surprised at the pleasant images it can evoke, given its freedom. Once, in a group relaxation session, I played my tape of the sounds of the sea to the participants in the third stage. After a while I noticed one lady wiping sweat from her brow with the back of her hand. After the session I pointed this out to her. She had been unaware of what she'd done but said she'd imagined she was lying on a tropical beach and had found it too hot. Such is the power of the mind.

When you have mastered the technique, you will find you can achieve some degree of relaxation almost anywhere. Five minutes spent really relaxing in the middle of a busy day can leave you revived for hours.

Hypnosis

Hypnosis is only a few steps away from deep relaxation. In order for it to be effective not only the body but also the mind must be relaxed and free, ready to receive suitable suggestions.

Self-hypnosis is a combination of hypnosis and relaxation whereby people are taught to relax themselves very deeply and then persuade themselves to do or feel things they are usually unable to manage. For example, shy people might be taught auto-hypnosis to make them bolder in certain situations. Training in self-confidence is called 'ego-strengthening'.

Self-hypnosis cannot be learnt from a book. There are commercially produced tapes available to help you do such things as diet and give up smoking. Their effectiveness varies greatly. Anyone seriously interested in the possibilities of hypnosis for their problems should seek the advice of a recognized hypnotherapist.

Other therapies

Other widely used methods for reducing tension and enhancing relaxation include yoga, meditation, aromatherapy and massage, to name but a few.

Many of these practices originated in the East, where people have for centuries recognized the importance of relaxation and harmonizing the workings of the body and the mind. In most areas there are classes for these activities at adult education centres, community centres, or privately. There are also numerous instruction books and tapes available to help you.

The effects of relaxation on the mind can be exhilarating in a peaceful way. All too often we tend to become afraid when mental calm descends, to feel 'unreal'. The feelings of calm and peaceful exhilaration should be welcomed and enjoyed, not feared and shunned.

Diet

While it is futile to worry about what you are unable to influence, you will feel less worried, depressed or anxious about something if you have power to influence the outcome, however minimally.

The very strong association between a sense of helplessness and clinical depression has been recognized for some time, and we believe that both the mentally and the physically ill benefit when they feel they are taking positive steps towards recovery rather than waiting passively for the doctors to do their work.

An extension of this self-help attitude is the idea that people should take positive steps to safeguard their health, to prevent themselves from becoming ill. Hence the exhortations to improve our eating habits, for example, by eating more fibre, less sugar and salt, and fewer additives.

Research has shown that just as there is a definite connection between diet and physical illness, so there is between diet and mental illness. For example, pellagra, an illness characterized by depression and dementia, is a result of a deficiency in niacin, part of the vitamin B complex.

In the same way that changes in the quantities of the various vitamins and minerals in the body can cause or alleviate mental illness, readjustment on a smaller scale can affect our day-to-day demeanour.

This daily influence can, of course, be positive or negative. By taking in too much of a substance our bodies do not require, we can make ourselves feel less animated than we should. Alternatively, we can improve our health and vitality by eating less of such substances and more of the foods we do need.

We can all improve our vitality simply by avoiding foods generally regarded as unhealthy, that is, foods containing added sugars, caffeine, alcohol, salt and artificial additives. Eating less, or preferably none, of these substances and replacing them with food such as fresh fruit and vegetables, wholemeal breads, lean meat and fish, will certainly make you feel more alive and energetic than you did before, and less susceptible to anxiety.

The effect is not instantaneous. If you have been consuming large quantities of unhealthy substances for a prolonged period, you may experience mild withdrawal symptoms if you give them up suddenly. These should not be severe, but could include headaches, irritability, a feeling of restlessness and a craving for the substances you are trying to give up. Such cravings are only your body's way of telling you of its deprivation. Although we tend to crave what our body finds itself missing, the things we crave are not necessarily good for us, as is the case with addictive substances – caffeine and sugar are included in this category. The withdrawal symptoms will last only a day or two and are not intolerable, especially if you keep in mind the feeling of well-being that will replace them.

Once weaned from unhealthy substances, you may notice cravings for healthy foods from time to time, which is your body's way of telling you of a possible chemical imbalance. I recall a story related to us as students about a little boy of three who was admitted to hospital for investigations because he kept eating salt, which in excess can be harmful. Tests showed that the child's body was failing to maintain the normal level of salt necessary for his body to function. His craving served to remedy this defect.

To take another example: I am at times a chocolate addict. Occasionally (and this is definitely *not* to be recommended) I have eaten nothing on a particular day but chocolate. The consequence of such debauchery is often that I feel edgy the following day. I become anxious more readily than usual. I also find I develop a craving for chicken, or bananas, or even orange juice because my body wishes to restore its chemical balance.

Some people take vitamin supplements. Large doses of vitamin B have been used to alleviate depression in some cases and relieve anxiety in others. Perhaps the best-known use of a vitamin B supplement is of B_6 to counteract the irritability and depression associated with pre-menstrual tension. It is often argued nowadays, however, that B_6 should be taken only as part of the entire vitamin B complex, in which the various elements complement one another. Pantothenic acid is believed to have a tension-relieving effect, and vitamin C is also useful for combating stress. Calcium too can calm, which may be why many people like to have a hot milk drink before going to bed (milk is rich in calcium). Bananas and potatoes contain traces of a chemical producing a calming effect.

Generally, a properly fed, properly exercised body will not need vitamin supplements just to stay healthy. Taking these to reduce stress should be done only on the instructions of a qualified medical practitioner.

The lesson for panic attack sufferers is clear. Eat the right foods and avoid those your body doesn't need, especially before anxiety-producing situations. If, for instance, you become very anxious before exams and one looms, take extra care to eat sensibly for a couple of weeks beforehand, and you will feel more alert and less jumpy.

Exercise

The benefits of a sensible balanced diet in improving mental efficiency and emotional control can be extended by exercise.

Think about it. The vast majority of adults in our society make very little use of their physical power. Our system works best when the two parts, mind and body, are cared for equally.

Any dog owner will vouch for the deterioration in the beloved pet's behaviour if it is not exercised regularly. Yet we fail to feel as much concern over our own lack of exercise.

Stress all too often builds up in those who spend too great a proportion of their time engaged in mental activity and take virtually no physical re-creation. Although, in our complex society, stress and emotional problems may not be avoidable, a physically toned individual is better able to cope.

As I said at the start of this book, the symptoms of fear were designed to prepare the system for physical action – fight or flight. Stress can be due to an accumulation of unresolved worries or one large worry. Exercise replaces the symptoms of stress and fear by providing the natural physical response. Physically fit people who take regular exercise will testify to feeling mentally invigorated afterwards, yet with a sense of calm and well-being.

Those whose anxiety is easily aroused are well advised to take more physical exercise. It must be emphasized, however, that suddenly to take up vigorous exercise after many years can be dangerous. Unfit muscles cannot resume where they left off – they must be gradually, very gradually, worked up to peak condition. This includes the heart, which is a muscle too. People who are overweight or who have any doubts about their physical condition must seek advice from their doctor before starting exercise.

Swimming is a safe form for most people. It exercises the large muscle groups without putting the sort of strain on the legs that jogging, for instance, may.

Again, it is not our purpose here to describe the pros and cons of the various forms of exercise. You will, though, notice a real improvement in your ability to cope with anxiety if you combine sensible eating – avoiding junk foods and stimulants such as caffeine and alcohol – with a programme of regular exercise that is suited to your age, build and general physical condition.

Such a lifestyle should be adopted gradually. To attempt to change overnight the habits of years may create more problems than it solves. Do it little by little. The further you progress, the less you will desire the 'unhealthy' foods and the more you will enjoy the exercise.

Reducing anxiety by problem-solving

One means of minimizing anxiety when you are facing difficulties is to confront them constructively. A woolly approach to problems usually serves only to increase uncertainty and anxiety. Instead of trying to defend yourself by running away from a difficulty you must go out and attack it. Any tactician knows that attack is the best form of defence.

Worriers will go around for days, or even weeks, with an unsolved problem churning away in the back of their head, raising their general background anxiety level, making them less efficient and perhaps even causing sleeplessness. All the while the problem is no nearer being solved.

Another typical worriers' response to a problem is to pick at random any solution that turns up without considering alternatives. This can prolong anxiety because you are likely to harbour subconscious doubt as to the wisdom of the decision. To solve a problem proceed as follows:

- Work out exactly what the crux of the problem is. Write it down at the top of a sheet of paper.
- Study it again to make sure that what you have written really is the core of your problem.

    There may be several interrelated problems of equal importance – if so, write them all down on separate sheets of paper. You may now choose which to work on first. If meanwhile ideas for tackling the other problems occur to you, note them on the appropriate headed sheets.

- Write down all the ways of tackling your problem that you can possibly think of – however ludicrous they may seem at first. This process may last minutes or weeks, depending on the nature of the problem and how much time you have. Never stop adding to your list simply because you think up one solution that appeals to you. The best ideas are not always the first ones.

I can call to mind at least two occasions in my life when a problem was solved using suggestions that at first seemed flippant or downright ridiculous. One of these involved the rest of the family. My husband and I were considering how best to extend our home to provide an extra bedroom and bathroom. The obvious solution was to build over the garage, but the cost proved to be prohibitive. In a fit of pique, my husband suggested our eldest son – who needed the extra room because he was unable to share amicably with his younger brother any longer – should sleep in the garage.

That apparently ridiculous suggestion slowly made sense and we ended up by converting the garage to provide the extra space and making a carport for our cars. All this cost less than half the estimate for the new construction.

- When you have listed every option you can think of, take each separately and consider its pros and cons. Although some solutions may have more points in favour than others, these will vary in import- ance. A solution with one overriding advantage may be preferable to another with half a dozen minor ones. Here is an example of how various options may be suggested to deal with a common family dilemma:

You and your spouse are planning your next holiday with your son, aged fif- teen, and your seventeen-year-old daughter.

Do you all go on holiday together?
Some families share similar interests, likes and dislikes and so are able to find a holiday that suits them all equally. This is, however, relatively rare, especially where teenage children are involved.

If you do wish to go on holiday together and your interests are not entirely compatible who is going to lose out? Is there is holiday complex that would cater for at least some of your interests? A compromise may be to spend part of the holiday in one place and part in another – if, for instance, some of you like the beach while others prefer cities and nightlife.

What are the alternatives?
First, you and your spouse can go on holiday alone. If so, what happens to
your son and daughter in your absence? Could they go at the same time on
holidays more suited to their own interests? Could they remain at home with
someone competent – a grandparent or other relative – to keep an eye on
things? Could you trust them to be left alone?

The range of possibilities is almost endless. These are the sort of questions
you should ask of many situations to ensure you're getting the best deal from
life. Too often we follow the same old path simply because it never occurs to
us to reconsider. Having gone through the exercise, you may discover that
the tried and tested way is still the best, and you'll appreciate it all the more
for having positively chosen it.

Panic attack sufferers may come to recognize some small areas provok-
ing anxiety that they'd not hitherto acknowledged. This could be something
as innocuous as a fear of going shopping in non-English-speaking countries
because of the difficulty of making themselves understood. This niggling
little worry has caused many people to fight shy of self-catering holidays
abroad which could have been admirably suitable in all other respects.

- Question all the rejected suggestions and honestly acknowledge the
  reasons for their rejection. This may even produce an easy way out of
  a dilemma; in the case I just mentioned, another member of your party
  who speaks the local language, or who is not embarrassed about trying, could do the shopping.

Lists
Making lists can serve to get worries 'off your chest'. If you are uneasy
about something, write it down and write down what you can do about it.
The very act of putting worries on paper makes them appear more manage-
able because they've become more tangible.

When you have a great deal to get done and worry about having enough
time to do it all, list every task. You will have great satisfaction crossing out
each one as it is completed. The eagerness to cross out another item will
also spur you on.

As has been shown often throughout this book, it is feelings of uncertainty
and the loss of ability to control your own destiny that provoke anxiety.
These can be significantly reduced by the positive approaches of confront-
ing worries and taking constructive steps towards solving them.

PART III
Help from friends

This third part of the book is aimed at telling panic attack sufferers and those near them how they may help one another. Until now I have aimed my advice mainly at the sufferer, because, in the end, only sufferers can cure themselves. Nevertheless, others may want and need to help. This section attempts to describe the most beneficial forms for that help to take. It also deals with the much-neglected area of panic attacks in children.

16
WHOM SHOULD YOU ASK FOR HELP?

I have shown, through case studies in earlier chapters, ways in which close relatives of panic attack sufferers can unwittingly make their symptoms worse. I shall now give positive advice as to what kind of help a panic attack sufferer might seek.

As a sufferer you may have been asked by people close to you what they should do to help you if you have a panic attack. Before advising you what to say I should like you to consider for a moment who should know about your panic attacks.

In the acute phase

Panic attack sufferers currently in the acute phase are unlikely to be going to work or socializing very much and will not be in close contact with many people apart from the immediate family. The acute phase should not last for more than a couple of months at the very most, probably much less. Although you will be feeling very agitated, unable to concentrate and worried, you should try to explain to whoever is looking after you exactly how you feel, especially when you feel panicky.

The attempt at explanation serves two very important purposes. In the first place it helps your companion to understand you better. Secondly, and perhaps more importantly from your point of view, the very act of trying to explain your feelings at that precise moment distances you from your panic and helps to break the panic attack spiral.

Many sufferers in the acute phase feel anxious at being left alone in the house for fear of panicking uncontrollably. A number of women I have treated have pleaded with their husbands to stay away from work so that they should not be left by themselves. This has often presented the husbands with a very difficult decision. If the husband does stay at home, it can cause financial and emotional strain at a time when a marriage is at its most vulnerable. It might be better to ask a close friend or relative who doesn't work to spend part of the day with you temporarily.

During the acute phase it is advisable to have someone close at hand to whom you can go for company when you feel panicky. But of course the more self-reliant you can be, the quicker you will recover.

Suzanne, whose case was described in Chapter 6, was afraid of being alone in the house all day. Her husband, although very sympathetic towards her, was unable to remain at home for fear of losing his job. Suzanne accepted this. Fortunately, she was very friendly with her next-door neighbour, who was aware of Suzanne's problem and willing to do all she could to help in this temporary crisis. Whenever Suzanne began to feel panicky alone at home, she would first of all try to distract herself by carrying out some household chores. Only if this failed would she go next door, where she would feel better for her neighbour's company.

I would advise anyone in the acute phase to follow Suzanne's example. If you have no one you can rely on locally, consider the possibility of someone coming to stay, just for a couple of weeks, to see you over the worst. If you do have a visitor, keep reminding yourself that it's only temporary and do your best to find ways of coping with panicky feelings yourself while the visitor's still there. Don't leave it until he or she has returned home to try. Moreover, I would suggest that your visitor doesn't remain with you at all times, but goes out from time to time, perhaps for ten minutes to the local shop, so that you can get used to being alone. It isn't advisable to have someone with you every moment of every day.

Should you be in a state of very severe anxiety and need a complete rest, your doctor might suggest that you be admitted to hospital for a short while. It will give you a very necessary break. A stay in hospital is nothing to fear – indeed, the thought of it will probably bring you a great deal of relief.

Spasmodic sufferers

As I noted earlier, panic attack sufferers in the acute phase are unlikely to venture far from home, so they will not have to explain their problems to anyone else, apart from their immediate family and any daytime companions. Spasmodic sufferers, however, will probably be living fairly normal, if somewhat restricted, lives. For you the question is how much to tell and to whom?

In general I would advise you to tell as few people as possible. This is not because there is anything to be ashamed of. But if you attempt to explain your trouble to everyone you met, you will merely reinforce your own opinion that you are different.

It is in the interests of spasmodic sufferers to believe themselves as normal as possible. They should constantly be attempting to overcome panics, ignoring the effects and behaving as normally as possible. If you see yourself as someone with a handicap, then you're less likely to make yourself behave normally. Whatever happens, you don't want others to begin to treat you as handicapped in some way because of your panics. If they do, you'll find that once you've overcome your panics and want to be treated normally again, it will take you a long time to get people to change their attitude towards you.

My advice would be to tell nobody of your spasmodic attacks unless you find yourself forced to go somewhere where you think you may succumb to feeling panicky. For example, I have never been happy about travelling on the underground. Some years ago, when I was a good deal less happy about it than now, I was in town for a conference with a friend from work. We were planning to travel by underground and, as I wasn't absolutely sure of my ability to cope fully, I thought I'd better warn her what might happen.

I explained that there was a slight possibility that I might feel panicky and dizzy on the train but that she shouldn't worry. I said I'd just leave the train at the next stop and sit down with my head on my knees until I felt better. It was fortunate I had told her this since there was one occasion when I did feel panicky. I did as I said and we resumed our trip. Had I not forewarned her, she might have worried needlessly and done something counter-productive.

If you find yourself in a similar situation, I suggest you explain very calmly and straightforwardly exactly what you would want your companion to do should you feel panicky. It's a sort of insurance, a way of preparing your escape route in advance just in case you need it.

17
CHILDREN
AND PANIC ATTACKS

Although children are unlikely to develop panic attacks themselves simply from having seen a close relative experience one, it isn't advisable to let children see you panic if it can reasonably be avoided. If it can't be avoided, then you should attempt to explain things as simply and calmly as possible. You could say, for example, that you feel unwell from time to time, but that you soon get better again, so it's nothing to worry about.

The important thing is not to alarm any children involved. If they see you coping fairly calmly and according to plan, then they'll model their attitudes on yours and will learn to react to their own anxieties in a similar way. If, on the other hand, you tend to become hysterical, your child might get frightened and come to regard you as some sort of invalid who has to be pandered to and tolerated.

A teenage son or daughter might benefit from a deeper understanding of your attacks, but don't try to make the family slaves to your disorder. Don't expect a great deal of extra attention just because of your panics. Your family may give it, but you shouldn't demand it if they don't.

Helping children with panic attacks
It is possible for children to have panic attacks. My own began when I was about ten years old. Whereas a teenager with panic attacks would benefit from reading this book and fully understanding what's involved, younger children should be handled differently. In most cases early action is the key. The answer to children's panics is to defuse the fear as early as possible.

When he was about eleven, Richard used to have to make a bus journey of about an hour each Saturday afternoon. He was accompanied by his thirteen-year-old brother and nine-year-old sister. The bus was usually crowded. The children often had to stand for at least part, if not all, of the journey. Although his brother and sister had always had a tendency to be travel-sick, Richard had never had this complaint.

One summer Saturday Richard remarked to me that he disliked the bus journey and was reluctant to go. On closer questioning I discovered that on the previous trip he had felt faint. He said it was very hot and stuffy on the bus and he'd been standing most of the way. On feeling faint he'd asked to sit down and had survived the journey. Now, however, he was fearing a recurrence.

It was important to provide Richard with a logical reason for having felt faint so that he could take practical steps to avoid it happening again. I pointed out that you can feel faint if you are too hot, and that he should take off his coat in the bus. I also told him to try standing near a door or an open window so that he got plenty of fresh air. I managed to convince him that his faintness was due to his being too hot. Whether or not this was actually true wasn't important. It was a very plausible explanation and could well have been the right one.

If Richard had been unable to accept a logical cause for his faintness, he'd have worried constantly that it might recur unexpectedly. Now that he knew why he had felt faint and what to do to stop it happening again, he was no longer afraid of the bus journey.

It is important to make the point here that I'm not saying that every child who feels faint is liable to have panic attacks. The fainting may have a physical cause and if you're in any doubt about this you should certainly consult your doctor.

Parents usually know their own children best. They can usually tell if that child is the sort to become anxious and worried about such things and liable to panic attacks. The way I handled Richard's case may not be the best way for your child; that's for you to decide. The main thing to convey, however, is that panic attacks are predictable and that they will go away if the right action is taken.

It is widely believed that phobias such as agoraphobia aren't experienced by children. Yet many do suffer from school phobia. They may be frightened of the journey to school or of standing in assembly, as I was myself.

Children who have panic attacks are often worried about going out alone and having nobody to turn to for help if they feel unwell. Many of these fears never surface because children aren't often expected to go out alone, except to school, hence school phobia.

Here are some guidelines for helping children with this complaint.

1. Give the child a plausible reason why the panic occurred so as to remove the unpredictability of another attack.
2. Offer the child a few practical things to do if it happens again.

Reassure the child by saying that all will be well if these things are done.

3. Try to make as little fuss as possible. Be very matter-of-fact in your explanations, yet reassuring.

4. If a child has experienced only one panic, try not to allow a similar situation to be avoided completely. If possible, see that the child is accompanied on the next occasion, without making a big issue of this. If everything is all right then, don't give praise or remind of former fears, but let the child go alone the next time.

5. If a child has experienced several panics and has developed a real fear of certain situations, allow those situations to be avoided for a while, provided they are not important, such as going to school.

6. If the child is afraid of feeling panicky at a particular time at school, try to alleviate this fear. For instance, if the child is afraid of school assembly, arrange with the head teacher that the child be excused for a period. The child will, it is hoped, later gain the confidence to resume. Forcing a child into a potential panic-arousing situation may well increase the anxiety to unacceptable levels and lead to the child's refusing to attend school at all. Another alternative to missing assembly altogether may be to sit near an exit with permission to leave if necessary, with no questions asked.

Children need to be helped to build up their confidence and to practise controlling their fears just as adult sufferers do. But because they haven't the power to run their own lives, parents must arrange for concessions to be made for them.

18
ADVICE TO
FRIENDS AND RELATIVES

We shall now turn our attention to ways in which close friends and relatives can help a panic attack sufferer. This chapter will, of course, also be useful to sufferers themselves.

Panic attack sufferers should try to be aware of the effects they have on those close to them. They should try to see themselves from other people's point of view so that they can understand the reactions of those people to their panics.

Although it is unpleasant to suffer from panic attacks, especially in the acute state, those who are emotionally involved with a sufferer will feel some anguish too. They will possibly feel incompetent and powerless, not knowing what to do to help. This may cause them to react in ways that might, on the face of it, appear hard.

Acute: apparent hostility

Remember the case of Betty (Chapter 7). Her husband was outwardly hostile towards her acute phase of panics. Even when she returned home from hospital for the weekend he went out and left her alone to cope with the children. Matters were resolved only when Betty seriously contemplated divorce. Only at this point did the couple really talk about their feelings.

It appeared that Betty's husband had become hostile and unhelpful because he felt frustrated and powerless to do anything to help her. This reaction is fairly common, especially between husbands and wives, yet it is frequently misinterpreted by panic attack sufferers as a lack of sympathy and understanding.

As a parent you may have become angry with a child who has just injured himself. Your anger is really frustration that the child is in pain, and you can't do anything to stop the pain. The same happens with close relatives of panic attack sufferers. This frustration and hostility is usually most common in the acute phase.

Spasmodic: be patient

During the spasmodic phase the most likely response of friends and relations is exasperation with a sufferer who doesn't appear to be doing all he or she can to cope with an attack. It is important at this stage to be patient. Sufferers must work things out at their own pace. To rush them will only delay progress.

Take the example of a suffering husband or wife who feels unable to accompany you on an evening out. Don't imagine that your partner is trying to spoil things for you. Try to go alone, but without bitterness. Don't try to punish the sufferer by taunting him or her with what he or she has missed when you get back. Don't, if you want your spouse to get better, try to arouse jealousy, as this can only increase the level of general anxiety.

By the same token, spasmodic sufferers should be prepared for their spouses to go out alone if they are unwilling to accompany them. Sufferers should accept the situation without reproaching their partners afterwards.

Going out together

If a sufferer decides to go out, despite feeling bad, then the companion should be watchful but not over-anxious. Try to engage the sufferer in conversation or draw attention to what is going on to distract any panicky feelings. If possible, agree beforehand what action you both will take should panic threaten. The sufferer might want to sit alone in the car, or take a walk outside with you or alone.

If you have agreed upon a course of emergency action before an outing, then you both should abide by it. If, for instance, you are going to the supermarket and have decided that the sufferer will try to do the shopping but that if he feels panicky, he will leave the trolley and wait in the car while you finish and pay, then that's what you will do. The sufferer should not expect to be driven home immediately, neither should you try to make him finish the shopping.

Sufferers must know that companions who are there to help will keep their word. Unreliable companions only create unnecessary extra anxiety for sufferers.

Checkpoints for helpers
1. Be supportive, keep your word, and don't expect progress to be very rapid.
2. Try not to reproach a sufferer with spoiling your life. This would create extra anxiety and make recovery slower.
3. Discuss your feelings about the problem, but talk positively, trying to find ways to resolve your differences.
4. Don't force sufferers to face a situation if they're not ready. They

must make their own choices about what to do and when for progress to be effective. Nevertheless, support them in what they decide.

5. Try not to allow your own life to become seriously disrupted. It's one thing to miss a television programme to help a sufferer with the shopping, but it's asking for trouble to take long periods of time off work.

   If you were, for instance, constantly staying at home when you should be at work, you might lose your job. You might then become very resentful of the sufferer for having messed up your life, and this resentment could grow into open hostility. Instead, you should do all you can to find someone to be on hand during the day, and call in yourself at lunchtimes perhaps, or telephone, to show that you care.

6. Sufferers need reassurance that they are still loved. If this reassurance is freely given, they will generally be less clinging and demanding.

7. Never fail to praise a sufferer's progress. Don't criticize lack of progress. Sufferers know themselves what they have failed to achieve and won't thank you for pointing it out.

8. Never remind a sufferer of past failures.

9. Finally, try not to make a sufferer feel an outsider because of the panics. Keep issuing invitations even if they have been declined before. With progress, they will begin to be accepted. They will also act as a challenge to the sufferer, and a reminder of what to aim for.

It isn't easy being an onlooker. It's very hard for non-sufferers to understand what all the fuss is about. It would be easy to say 'Snap out of it!' If you do feel frustrated with it at times, go away somewhere and stamp your feet or beat your pillow alone. Don't throw your frustrations in the face of the one you're trying to help, as this might provoke extra anxieties. Try to keep a sense of humour. Try to laugh *with*, not *at*, the sufferer.

19
LOOSEN UP
AND LOOK AGAIN

By now I hope that you are feeling excited at the prospect of that new life, which is yours for the taking. Don't rush things – be patient. It will take time to re-examine your habitual responses and reactions, the ways you behave and the things you think, which is what you must do to change your life and free yourself from panic.

Do you worry uselessly? Do you hold honest, up-to-date mental images of those important to you? Do you see the bad side automatically when you could learn to see the good? It is possible that many of your responses and reactions will remain the same after your re-analysis. But some, undoubtedly, will be updated. This is the time when you can start getting to know more about yourself, learning in greater depth about your personality. You should be able to do this more easily since you have been practising the techniques I have described in this book.

A new image of yourself
I shall describe a method, which was devised by an American named George Kelly, of helping you loosen up your image of yourself, your self-concept. Chart 1 lists the people who may have been important in your life. Write their names in the spaces provided. The first two will probably be 'mother' and 'father', unless you weren't brought up by your own parents.

Now turn to Chart 2. Fill in the names as they correspond to the letters *a* to *i* in Chart 1. Now take the first line of names and write down any personal quality, good or bad, that comes to mind when you think of them. This is usually done by asking yourself in what way any two of them are similar. For instance, you might think two of them are generous. Write 'generous' in the space provided. Put only one quality for each group of three, so choose the most striking one each time. These are the qualities of the people most important to you, and they will have a significant bearing on your view of yourself.

When you have completed your list of qualities, giving a different one each time, turn to Chart 3. List each quality from Chart 2 and next to it write what you consider to be its opposite. Put the most desirable qualities on the left and the less desirable or undesirable ones on the right. For example, if one of the qualities on Chart 2 was 'beautiful', you might consider the opposite to be 'ugly'. You would then put 'beautiful' on the left and 'ugly' on the right, assuming that you would rather be beautiful than ugly.

The seven dots in between the two ends of the scale provide you with a seven-point rating for each quality. Your next step is to place yourself, as you see yourself *now,* somewhere on each scale. Place a cross on the appropriate dot.

Now consider your ideal self, the person you would like to be if you could. Put a circle for your ideal self on one of the seven dots on each line. The circles may coincide with the crosses. You can now see at a glance which qualities you desire to change most: they are the ones with the biggest space between the circle and the cross. You have a concrete plan of what you're aiming for.

If you want to go a step further, you can now take each quality in turn and consider how you might improve and become more and more as you want to be. What aspects of your behaviour and thinking do you need to change? Try to give yourself some real life instances if you can.

You can discover a little more about yourself by asking yourself questions about the space between the circles and the crosses. Suppose one of your lines reads 'beautiful' – 'ugly', and you want to be more beautiful than you are. You then ask yourself why. If the answer is, 'So that people will like me', ask yourself, 'Why do I want people to like me?' and then 'Why do I think people will like me only if I'm beautiful?' Continue making each of your answers into another question in this way until you cannot give any more answers. Make a note of your final answer and repeat this process with each of the other qualities in turn. You will find that many of your final answers are the same. These answers will give you a clue as to the driving forces in your life.

This exercise isn't always easy to do at first. If you can't get anywhere alone, try it with a friend. Its purpose is to get you to reconsider your views of yourself and others, to loosen up your attitudes and opinions, and to examine them to see if they are still valid or if they have become outdated and need revising.

You may be wondering why you are asked to derive your list of qualities from a list of people who have been important in your life, rather than just thinking up a list. The reason is this: we all see the world and the other people in it in terms of what is important to us. Consider for a moment the person who has a complex about having a large nose. This person believes that everyone notices his nose immediately, and spends a great deal of time worrying about it. That same person will, you can be sure, notice the size and shape of every nose he or she meets. Do the rest of us ever take that much notice of other people's noses? Similarly, the eternal dieter will always notice whether a new acquaintance is too fat or slim, almost to the inch.

The same thing happens with personality characteristics. We see in others those qualities, or lack of them, which we regard as important. We see the world through our own eyes, influenced by our own aspirations and fears. None of us judges the world dispassionately and objectively. Each of us sees something different, given the same thing to look at. Therefore, the list of qualities that you deduced from your list of characters reflected qualities important to you. Another person who knew those same people would probably produce a different list of qualities, those important to him. It is our minds and the interpretation we put on people, places and events that shape our lives, not the people, places and events themselves.

I hope you learn how to control your mind and make it work for you rather than against you, as it has done during your panics. I wish you courage, enthusiasm and success. Seize your opportunities when they appear. Go out and find them, don't sit about waiting.

CHART 1

Make sure you give a different name for each description.

a Your mother or the person who brought you up ......
b Your father or father-figure...........................
c Your brother or sister (the most significant one if you
   have several) or a childhood friend if you're an only
   child ....
d Your best friend.......................................
e Your husband or wife, or your closest friend if you're
   single...
   ....
f Someone you admire or have admired at some point
   in your life, real or fictional.........................
g Someone who let you down..............................
h Someone you dislike, real or fictional.................
i A teacher at school ....

CHART 2

Write the names corresponding to the letters in Chart 1 in the spaces provided on each row. In the last column, put down the quality suggested by the three names in that line. Make sure each quality you list is different.

	Names			**Quality**
a c e	....	....	....	....
b d f	....	....	....	....
a d g	....	....	....	....
b g i	....	....	....	....
g h a	....	....	....	....
f d c	....	....	....	....
e a h	....	....	....	....
e g c	....	....	....	....

Example
a b c	Mum	Dad	Mary	beautiful
	....	....	....	....

CHART 3

Write down the qualities from Chart 2 and what you consider to be the opposite of each, putting the desirable quality on the left and the undesirable one on the right.

The dots between the extremes are a scale. Put a cross on one dot on each line to indicate where on the scale you believe you fall yourself. Now go back and put a circle on each line where you would like to be.

Desirable Undesirable

1. .... • • • • • • • ....

2. .... • • • • • • • ....

3. .... • • • • • • • ....

4. .... • • • • • • • ....

5. .... • • • • • • • ....

6. .... • • • • • • • ....

7. .... • • • • • • • ....

8. .... • • • • • • • ....

Example
            Beautiful   ugly
.... • • ◎ • • X • ....

CHECKLIST FOR
PANIC ATTACK SUFFERERS

The preceding pages contain a great deal of information which will take time to digest and fully understand. To help you and to provide a quick reference for refreshing your memory the main points of the book are summarized here.

1. If you are in an acute phase of panic attacks try to be positive and patient. Seek professional help if you feel you need it, and try to avoid panic-inducing situations for the time being.
   Stop at this point until you are over the acute phase.

2. If you are in a *spasmodic phase* begin now to consider your plan. List what you want to do that you can't do now. Begin to consider easy stages to your goal.

3. Accept the responsibility for your own progress.

4. Make it clear to close family and friends what you want them to do and, perhaps more importantly, what you'd prefer them not to do.

5. If you previously endured an acute phase consider what caused it. It was probably a combination of events. Are these events likely to repeat themselves? If so, are they avoidable or should you consider changing your attitude towards them to a more positive one?

6. Seriously consider beginning to change your way of life to reduce your susceptibility to anxiety or stress. Changes that would be beneficial include eating healthier food, drinking less alcohol, giving up smoking, taking regular physical exercise and practising some form of relaxation.

7. Look forward, not back.

USEFUL ADDRESSES

Self-help groups

The following self-help groups may be approached if you feel you need to contact others with anxieties similar to your own. Please enclose a stamped self-addressed envelope if writing to them.

Alcoholics Anonymous
PO Box 1
Stonebow House
Stonebow
York YO1 2NJ
Tel: 01904 644026
or 0171 352 3001 (London area)

Compassionate Friends (for
    bereaved parents whose child
    of any age has died)
53 North Street
Bristol BS3 1EN
Tel: 01272 539639

Cruse (help for the bereaved)
Cruse House
126 Sheen Road
Richmond
Surrey TW9 1UR
Tel: 0181 940 4818

Cry-sis (support for parents of
    consistently crying babies)
BM Cry-sis
London WC1N 3XX
Tel: 0171 404 5011

Depressives Associated (support for
    sufferers and relatives)
PO Box 5
Castle
Portland
Dorset DT5 1BQ

Parents Anonymous (problems with
    children or to help those tempted
    to abuse their children)
6-7 Manor Gardens
London N7 6LA
Tel: 0171 263 8818

Phobic Action *(support for those with phobias and anxieties)*
Greater London House
547-551 High Road
Leytonstone
London E11 4PR
Tel: 0181 558 3463/6012

Samaritans *(Head Office)*
10 The Grove
Slough
Berks SL1 1QP
Tel: 01753 532713
(For local branch see your own phone book)

The addresses above are just a few voluntary groups to whom readers of this book might feel the need to turn. There are many others, including those set up to provide psychological support for those anxious about various medical ailments. The addresses of these, and othres may be found in *The Voluntary Agencies Directory*, published by Bedford Square Press, and available for consultation in the reference section of large public libraries.

Books

Relaxation and Meditation Techniques, Leon Chaitow (Thorsons Publications, 1983)
Encyclopaedia of Natural Medicine, Michael Murray and Joseph Pizzorno (Optima, 1990)

Tapes

A selection of tapes suitable for meditation and relaxation are available from

Dawn Awakening
PO Box 15
Newton Abbot
Devon TQ12 6XE
Tel: 01626 682427
(send s.a.e. for catalogue)

My own personal favourites are: 'Breathe' - a relaxing meditative instrumental musical journey. 'Restful Sounds' - the ocean on one side and an English garden on the other. There is also 'Garden of Dreams' which contains rainfall which many people find relaxing.

Other addresses

Association of Chartered Clinical Psychologists in Private Practice (ACCPIPP) For those seeking qualified psychological treatment on a non-NHS basis.
Tel: 0171 937 9267 for names of local practitioners.

British Society of Experimental and Clinical Hypnosis (BSECH) For those seeking treatment for qualified psychologists who use hypnosis if appropriate.
Contact Dr Michael Heap for names of local practitioners at:
The Centre for Psychotherapeutic Studies
University of Sheffield
16 Claremont Crescent
Sheffield S10 2TA
Tel: 01742 824970

British Wheel of Yoga
Grafton Grange
Grafton
York YO5 9QQ
Tel: 01901 23386

INDEX

life events, stressful, 90–2
lists, 104
loss of control, 47–8
loss of identity, 48–9, 88–9, 91
love, falling in, 68

marital problems, 58
massage, 99
meditation, 99
memory lapses, 11–12
men, alcoholism, 49
mental blocks, 11–12
'mental set', 78–9
minerals, 100
modelling, phobias, 42–3
motivation, overcoming panic attacks, 66–7

nausea, 14
nervous breakdowns, 13

panic attacks: acute phase, 33–5, 65, 107–8, 113; acute-spasmodic phase, 37–40, 67; avoiding, 25–7; case history questionnaire, 60–2; children and, 21–2, 43, 110–12; coping techniques, 73–81; development of, 22–4; direct influence of significant others, 43–5; effects on daily life, 21; escape from, 56–9, 75–7, 80; first causes, 19–21; help from friends, 105–9, 113–15; indirect influence of significant others, 45; normal and abnormal panics, 13–14; overcoming, 63–104; panic attack spiral, 27–9, 28; patterns of, 33–41; personality of sufferer, 49–55; recognizing, 17–18; remission, 67–70; spasmodic phase, 35–7, 65–7, 108–9, 114–15; spasmodic-acute phase, 40–1, 67; staying panic-free, 87–9; symptoms, 11, 14, 65–7; triggers, 25, 27–9
personality, 30, 49–55
phobias: desensitization, 16–17; modelling, 42–3; school phobia, 22, 111–12; specific, 16–17, 18, 42–3; see also agoraphobia
positive thinking, 53–4, 77–8, 80
potential escape, 76, 80

problem-solving, 102–4
progress charts, 85–6
punishments and rewards, 46–7

Rahe, R. H., 90
relaxation, 16–17, 58–9, 69, 88, 92–9; shoppers' relaxation, 75, 76, 80, 85
remission, 67–70
retirement, 91
reversal theory, 58–9, 88
rewards and punishments, 46–7

school phobia, 22, 111–12
self-concept, 116–20
self-confidence, 99
self-hostility, 46–8, 49
self-hypnosis, 99
self-pity, 77
self-reliance, 69–70
self-respect, 83
shoppers' relaxation, 75, 76, 80, 85
shopping, supermarkets, 76–7, 78, 84, 85, 114
significant others, 43–5
social drinking, 74–5
social phobias, 14, 15–16, 21, 22
spasmodic panic attacks, 35–7, 65–7, 108–9, 114–15
spasmodic-acute attacks, 40–1, 67
specific phobias, 42–3
state anxiety, 31, 32
stress, 12–13, 65, 87, 90–2, 101
strong mindedness, 54–5
supermarkets, 76–7, 78, 84, 85, 114
symptoms, 65–7

thinking, positive, 77–8, 80
thought stopping, 80
trait anxiety, 30, 31
tranquillizers, 37, 73–4
triggers, 25, 27–9

Valium, 73
vision, blurred, 14
vitamins, 100, 101
vomiting, 22

women, agoraphobia, 48–9
worry, 87–8, 102

yoga, 99

Other personal development titles available from Vermilion

ALL IN THE MIND?
Brian Roet

Have you a problem that won't go away? This book offers a key to solving long-term problems, physical, social and emotional. Drawing on his practical experience, Dr Roet shows how the mind plays a major role in causing and maintaining illness, and how many physical and psychological symptoms are messages from the unconscious.

PERSONAL THERAPY
Brian Roet

In this book Dr Roet shows us how we can use therapeutic techniques can be used to release deep-seated emotions, acknowledge our strengths and weaknesses and establish emotional equilibrium. His reassuring and practical advice guides us towards new ways to enjoy a more fulfilling life.

BE ASSERTIVE
Beverley Hare

Beverley Hare dispels the myth that assertive behaviour is aggressive, and draws on her own experience to explain how becoming more assertive can help us all to improve the quality of relationships, both in the business environment and in our personal lives.

SEX: HOW TO MAKE IT BETTER FOR BOTH OF YOU
Martin Cole and Windy Dryden

Written by two highly experienced therapists this book presents the facts about sex and sex therapy in a readable and accessible style, offering practical and reassuring help.

ANXIETY AND DEPRESSION
Professor Robert Priest

Professor Priest has written this book to provide help for those feeling anxious and depressed. He covers practical self help methods of reducing stress and offers an explanation of the causes and effects of anxiety and depression. This book provides up-to-date information on the professional help available and details the action and side effects of medication.

DIY PSYCHOTHERAPY
Martin Shepard

Would you like to understand yourself better? Dr Shepard draws on his long experience as a professional therapist to present this do-it-yourself approach to psychotherapy. Each chapter focuses on one aspect of human behaviour and concludes with a series of exercises designed to give you a clearer understanding of your own thoughts and responses.

The following titles are also available from Vermilion. To order your copy direct (p+p free), use the form below or call our credit-card hotline on **01279 427203**.

Please send me

...... copies of **ALL IN THE MIND?** by Brian Roet @ £8.99 each

...... copies of **PERSONAL THERAPY** by Brian Roet @ £8.99 each

...... copies of **SEX: HOW TO MAKE IT BETTER FOR BOTH OF YOU** by Martin Cole & Windy Dryden @ £8.99 each

...... copies of **PANIC ATTACKS** by Sue Breton @ £8.99 each

...... copies of **ANXIETY AND DEPRESSION** by Professor Robert Priest @ £8.99 each

...... copies of **DIY PSYCHOTHERAPY** by Dr Martin Shepard @ £8.99 each

Mr/Ms/Mrs/Miss/Other (Block Letters)

....

Address...

....

....

Postcode............................Signed.......................................

HOW TO PAY

☐ I enclose a cheque/postal order for £...
made payable to 'Vermilion'

☐ I wish to pay by Access/Visa card (delete where appropriate)

Card Number ☐☐☐☐☐☐☐☐☐☐☐☐☐☐☐☐

Expiry Date ☐☐☐☐

Post order to **Murlyn Services Ltd, PO Box 50, Harlow, Essex CM17 0DZ**.

POSTAGE AND PACKING ARE FREE. Offer open in Great Britain including Northern Ireland. Books should arrive less than 28 days after we receive your order; they are subject to availability at time of ordering. If not entirely satisfied return in the same packaging and condition as received with a covering letter within 7 days. Vermilion books are available from all good booksellers.